The Spirit and the Bride say Come!

Debbie Hicks

NEEDLE ROCK
PRESS

Visit Needle Rock Press at www.needlerockpress.com

The Spirit and the Bride say Come!
Copyright © 2022 Debbie Hicks

Cover designed by Taylor Bates of New Melody Art Design.
Copyright © 2022 Taylor Bates
www.instagram.com/taytaygumby
Original photo licensed from MNStudio on AdobeStock

Interior Design by Sandy Cathcart
www.scatsandycathcart.com

All rights reserved. No portion of this book may be reproduced, stored in a retrieval system, or transmitted in any form or by any means-- electronic, mechanical, photocopy, recording, scanning, or other--except for brief quotations in critical reviews or articles, without the prior written permission of the publisher.

Unless otherwise indicated, all Scripture quotations are taken from the New King James Version®. Copyright © 1982 by Thomas Nelson. Used by permission. All rights reserved.

Scripture quotations marked NASB have been taken from the New American Standard Bible, Copyright © 1960, 1962, 1963, 1968, 1971, 1972, 1973, 1975, 1977, 1995 by The Lockman Foundation, Used by permission. All rights reserved.

Scripture quotations marked NIV are taken from the Holy Bible, New International Version®, NIV® Copyright ©1973, 1978, 1984, 2011 by Biblica, Inc.® Used by permission. All rights reserved worldwide.

Scripture quotations marked KJV are taken from the King James Version, Public Domain.

Published in the United States by Needle Rock Press
341 Flounce Rock Rd.

Prospect, OR 97536

Needle Rock Press books may be purchased in bulk for ministry purposes by contacting sandycathcart@gmail.com

ISBN: 978-1-943500-24-6 (paperback)
ISBN: 978-1-943500-25-3 (ebook)

To my two amazing children,
Jonathan and Bethany,
who willingly followed me on this bumpy journey
even when we didn't know where we were going.

Jonathan and Bethany
were in the streets sharing their faith
and serving the lost
when most kids were at soccer practice.

Thank you both!
I have never been prouder to call you my own.

Love, Mom

Contents

Introduction vii
Prologue ix

PART ONE—THE VISION
1. The Birth of a Vision 1
2. The Vision Comes Together 5
3. The Vision Comes Alive 13
4. The Vision Goes to the Streets....................... 21

PART TWO—THE BRIDE'S INVITATION
5. The Bride Comes out of the Closet............... 33
6. The Bride Goes into the Darkness 41
7. The Bride Seeks the Lost 47
8. The Bride Takes Part in Halloween Night..... 55

PART THREE—THE BRIDE'S JOURNEY
9. Into All the World 63
10. Bridal Love 69
11. Amsterdam 73
12. Spreading the Vision 79

PART FOUR—THE BRIDE'S DISCOVERY
13. Out of the Mouths of Babes 85
14. She is a Lily.. 93
15. Las Vegas, Dying for Love 99
16. Out of Africa 107

PART FIVE—THE BRIDE'S JOY

17. Bridal Boutique 113
18. Jerusalem 125
19. The Bridegroom 135
20. Going Forward 141

    Invitation 144
    Acknowledgments 145
    About the Author 147
    Contact **148**

Introduction

Now and then, someone comes along who reminds us we were created for greatness. Such a person's charisma touches us in such a way that our souls gain the courage to step out and fly. Not just fly—but soar above the mundane and ordinary as we bask in the breath of God.

Debbie Hicks is that person in my life.

When I was just a new believer, I learned from Debbie's boldness that my awesome Creator Redeemer still does the miraculous—and that He does those miracles through ordinary people like me.

"We give him our little loaves and fishes," Debbie said to me, "and then God multiplies them."

I've never forgotten those words.

Now, many decades later, I'm still seeing the fruit of her words as I continue to give God my loaves and fishes.

What loaves and fishes will you give Him?

Pray before reading this book and ask God to show you what loaves and fishes you have to give. Then, as you read the amazing experiences of this extraordinary woman, see what sparks excitement in your soul. Write it down, then pray for the strength and courage to carry it out.

If you would like to talk with someone about what you have discovered, email me at sandycathcart@gmail.com

May the peace of God and the fire of the Holy Spirit ignite a fire of passion in you today!

    Sandy Cathcart

    www.scatsandycathcart.com

If even one person "gets" Debbie's creative, powerful message of Jesus Christ's love and passion for His Bride, then God will be glorified. This book of exciting, life-changing, first-hand, first-tried adventures in reaching the lost will inspire you to join Debbie with a fresh perspective of Jesus Christ's love for us, His Bride, His Church.

    Kathy Smith

Prologue

"My answer to you, Debbie," my friend said, "is a big 'Yes!' Truly, Halloween night is a real harvest party in the true sense of the word. How else could you get thousands of people who don't know Jesus all standing in the same place?"

I took his advice and attended my first Halloween Festival. Ashland is a great theater town, so the costumes were unbelievably real. Every type of costume you could imagine was there in full glory.

I was passing out my invitations when I suddenly came face-to-face with the devil! He even had what looked like real horns protruding out of his forehead.

As the man approached, he looked me in the eyes and calmly said, "I know who you are."

"Oh, you do. Who am I?"

"You are the Bride of Christ."

I took a small step back. "How do you know?"

"I'm the devil," he said. "I know these things."

And then he turned and was gone.

Part 1

The Vision

1

The Birth of a Vision

No Ordinary Dream

IT WAS EARLY MORNING. I was half awake and half asleep. I'm not sure if it was a dream or a vision, but at the time, I thought it was real.

I saw a stunning bride standing alone in the middle of a beautiful park. She wore a wedding gown similar to the one Princess Diana wore for her wedding. The bride was smiling at me and holding an enormous bouquet. It seemed as if the aroma of roses filled my bedroom. She was giving me some kind of invitation.

How strange, I thought, but I didn't have to think further, because it was spring vacation, and my children were already calling me. Besides, what could this dream, or vision, or whatever it was, possibly have to do with me?

Not Once, But Twice

A year later, I had the dream again. Or was it a vision? I'll never be quite sure. I saw the same bride in the same park wearing the same beautiful dress and holding the same bouquet, but she was a year older.

I was bewildered. Once might be a fluke, but twice?

It seemed to me that this bride was frozen in time, waiting and hoping that I would wake up and remember seeing her. What did she want?

The dream seemed so real. Was God trying to speak to me?

I had a powerful urge to tell someone to see if they thought God might be speaking to me. But how could I find the words to explain? My husband Clyde should be the best person to listen to me, but I worried he wouldn't take me seriously. It all seemed so strange.

I fretted all morning and into the afternoon. Then I finally concluded I had to be willing to let go of the dream, or vision, or whatever it was, if no one else understood.

So, I did what all women do in such a situation. I prepared Clyde an extraordinary dinner of his favorite tacos.

When he was happy and full, and the children were off playing, I quietly told him about my vision and how I had now seen the exact thing twice.

To my surprise, he listened intently while his gray eyes sparkled with curiosity. Then he said, "I think you should talk with one of our pastors."

I nearly jumped out of my chair with excitement! Could it really be God was speaking to me? And in such a way? In a way that He had spoken to the prophets of old.

Thus, I began an amazing journey that ended up taking me halfway around the world and shaking up my life as nothing else could. It was the birth of a vision and also the birth of hope. It was the first time I realized God still speaks to his people in amazing ways. And it was the first time I took a small step toward something enormous, trembling as I went, but finding God to be utterly faithful.

Did you know THERE IS GOING TO BE a GREAT WEDDING in HEAVEN?

Revelation 19:7-8 "Let us rejoice and be glad and give the glory to Him, for the marriage of the Lamb has come and His bride has made herself ready. It was given to her to clothe herself in fine linen, bright and clean; for the fine linen is the righteous acts of the saints. NASU

You are invited to be in that wedding!

The BIBLE says that GOD'S ONLY SON, JESUS CHRIST, is preparing a BRIDE to LIVE and REIGN WITH HIM in HEAVEN.

Ephesians 5:25-28. Christ loves the church and gave Himself up for her, so that He might sanctify her, having cleansed her by the washing of water with the word, that He might present to Himself the church in all her glory, having no spot or wrinkle or any such thing; but that she would be holy and blameless. NASU

The BIBLE SAYS that JESUS LOVES THOSE who BELIEVE in HIM LIKE a GROOM LOVES HIS BRIDE.

He gives His life for us. **Romans 5:6-8**
He prepares us for heaven. **Ephesians 5:26**
He will come and get us. **John 14:2-3**

If you turn from your sins and believe in Jesus Christ, you will be added to those who are loved and saved by His wonderful Grace, and you will spend eternity in heaven with Him.

John 3:16. "For God so loved the world, that He gave His only begotten Son, That whoever believes in Him shall not perish, but have eternal life. NASU

The Bride of Christ

The Spirit and the Bride Say Come

Let us be glad and rejoice, and give honor to Him:
For the marriage of the Lamb is come, and his wife hath made herself ready.

And to her was granted that she should be arrayed in fine linen, clean and white: for the fine linen is the righteousness of saints.

And He saith unto me, Write, Blessed are they that which are called unto the marriage supper of the Lamb. And He saith unto me, these are the true sayings of God.

Rev. 19:7-9

And the Spirit and the bride say, Come. And let him that heareth say, Come. And let him that is athirst come. And whosoever will, let him take the water of life freely.

Rev. 22:17

Why not make absolutely certain of heaven by opening your heart to Christ the Savior and Lord. Right now, inviting Him to enter, to cleanse it from sin, and to make it His permanent dwelling place? He gives us this assurance:

...If anyone hears My voice and opens the door, I will come in to him, and dine with him, and he with Me.

Rev. 3:20

(Who was — — — and is — — — and is to come.)
Rev. 4:8

2

The Vision Comes Together

Sharing the Vision

CLYDE ENCOURAGED ME to speak with one of our pastors regarding the vision. I was thrilled to think that God might actually be speaking to me. Rick, the associate pastor, listened intently and said I should talk to Jon, our senior pastor. Jon gave me permission to stand in front of our church that very night and share it.

I couldn't believe it. I was nervous and excited and scared at the same time.

I will never forget that night when I stood in front of the congregation trying to explain something I didn't truly understand myself.

At that point, I could claim nothing but simple obedience, so I got up in front of all those people and told them what I saw, even though I was given no course at the time of what to follow. I just knew I had to find a dress and a bride to wear it.

I found out later that after I shared my vision that night, it created a bit of a stir for some people. One woman told me she and her husband got in a fight on the way home. Her husband thought I made no sense at all while she thought I did.

It's funny. Looking back, I realize it was the last time our church opened the floor to share visions.

A Life of Its Own

The very next day, Friday, the vision began to take on a life of its own. I attended a women's Bible study every Friday morning. On this particular day, a woman I had never met came up to me following the meeting.

"I own a bridal shop," she said. "I recently sold my shop and gave all my dresses away except for one very special dress." Her blue eyes sparkled with excitement. "I want to give it to you!"

I was so excited that I grabbed her and gave her a big hug.

When Clyde and I had married, I didn't have a dress of my own. I had borrowed one from a classmate. It seemed utterly impossible that I could own a wedding dress. Even if I could find one, how could I pay for it? And here was this lady, who didn't even know me, offering to give me a beautiful dress.

I love God's timing. It has a beautiful flow. You can almost taste His will when you're in it.

Looking back, the interesting part is that I got my first wedding dress at a wedding. A good friend of ours was getting married at our church the very next day, and the kind lady said she would meet me there with my first wedding dress.

The Dress

The next day, I arrived at the wedding excited and happy for the bride and groom, but also ecstatic to think I would be getting my own wedding dress very soon. As I sat in the church watching our friends exchange their vows, my mind kept jumping ahead, wondering what in the world was God up to? And, how in the world did I get in the middle of it?

Just before the reception, my new friend came up to me. "Here it is."

She held up a dress that was every bit as beautiful as the one I had seen in my vision. Tears flooded my eyes as she handed it to me. I carried the wedding dress out to my car, where I gently laid it over the seat. Then I raced back to the reception, thinking, *today I will find the bride who will wear this gorgeous gown.*

As I walked into the reception hall, I scanned the crowd looking for the most beautiful girl. When I spotted her, I boldly walked up and began to say, "You—" but before I could go further, I clearly heard God say, *No.*

I clumsily finished the sentence, "You . . . have a very beautiful dress.

Then I turned and began walking away. I was thinking, *Oh my goodness, this is really happening. I am not to pick the bride. God is going to pick the bride!*

I felt as if I was walking on holy ground.

The Bride

About a week later, I entered our church coffee shop to meet a friend. As I walked in, I saw this beautiful girl wearing an apron and carrying two huge buckets of ice. She looked just like she had stepped out of the Bible—Rebecca going to water the camels. I had seen her often in our Bible study. She had such a sweet countenance that it was easy to see she was a lover of God.

I think she recognized me, because she began to walk toward me as I walked toward her. With complete confidence, I looked at her, "I think you might be the bride."

Tears welled up in her eyes. "God told me that very thing, but I was afraid to tell anyone I thought God was calling me."

We immediately grabbed each other into a big hug while tears streamed down our faces. Melissa and I absolutely knew God was calling us into something way bigger than either of us could ever imagine.

Later, when I brought her the dress, it fit like a glove. How was that even possible? Melissa was stunning beyond belief.

I would soon learn that there is something enormously powerful about putting on a wedding dress. I saw it happen numerous times at the bridal shop I started a few years later when each woman tried on a wedding dress. It was as if this magical transformation had occurred within the woman. You could see it in her eyes, on her face, in her countenance, and in the way she held herself.

When Melissa put on the dress, and it fit perfectly, we both felt as if this ministry must be much bigger than we could possibly imagine. We knew it was totally from God, and we were just along for the ride.

The Invitation

Clyde and I now had a beautiful Bride in a gorgeous wedding gown, and I was slowly getting little glimpses of what I believed Jesus was saying to me concerning the vision. Those of us who have placed our trust in Jesus are His Bride. We have been made righteous through the shedding of His blood, and through His resurrection, we have become sons and daughters of God. Because Jesus died for our sins, we are now white as snow (See Isaiah 1:18).

God was clearly calling us out into the world to share the good news of his coming.

After much thought and prayer, we decided we needed to give our Bride a voice in the form of an invitation. We wanted the invitations to be different than the average tracts Christians were handing out, because such tracks were recognizable a mile away and had lost their mystery. So, to keep people curious, we decided to use scripture from Revelation about the Bride of Christ.

Instead of a booklet, we used a beautiful font on brown parchment paper. We rolled the paper like a scroll and fastened it with a little gold ring. It turned into an alluring mystery. People were curious about what we were inviting them to. It turned out to be the perfect invitation to our heavenly wedding.

So now, we had a pretty good understanding of what was next. We had the Bride, we had her invitation, and now we needed to find the park I had seen in the vision.

The Spirit and the Bride say Come!"

Let us be glad and rejoice, and give honour to him:
For the marriage of the Lamb is come,
and his wife hath made herself ready.

And to her was granted that she should be arrayed in fine linen,
clean and white: for the fine linen is the righteousness of saints.

And he saith unto me, Write, Blessed are they which are called
unto the marriage supper of the Lamb.
And he saith unto me, These are the true sayings of God.
—Revelation 19:7-9 (KJV)

And the Spirit and the bride say, Come! And let him that heareth
say, Come. And let him that is athirst come. And whosoever will,
let him take the water of life freely.
—Revelation 22:17 (KJV)

Why not make absolutely certain of Heaven
by opening your heart to Christ, the Savior and Lord?
Right now, invite Him to enter, to cleanse it from sin,
and to make it His personal dwelling place.
He gives us this assurance:

If anyone hears My voice and opens the door,
I will come in to him and dine with him, and he with Me.
—Revelation 3:20

Who was - - - and is - - - and is to come!
—Revelation 4:8

3

The Vision Comes Alive

Jesus Freaks

I GAVE MY LIFE TO JESUS CHRIST in my early twenties. In doing so, I was a part of the outpouring of the Holy Spirit that people now refer to as the Jesus Movement. I was one of those radical hippies who was rebellious as the day was long. We were dropouts of society living in hippie communes all across northern California.

People called us Jesus freaks back in those days. It was common for us to stand on street corners and hand out tracts, freely sharing our testimonies of how God saved such a wild group as ourselves. Although I was part of the group, most of my friends were non-believers, because my contact with the world was still pretty strong. I remember when I heard the word "potluck" at a gathering for the first time. I had no idea it meant to bring food. I spent the whole evening wondering where the "Pot" was!

In my walk with Jesus, I've observed that the more I began to walk in the light, I naturally had less and less contact with the world. Looking back, I think I was more profitable spiritually in my early years because I was still around lots of people who didn't know Jesus. As I quit going to clubs and parties, I had less contact with my old friends.

I hardly ever talked to non-believers because I felt out of step with them. Instead, I began surrounding myself with believers. I was basking in my newfound family, meeting in fellowship, going to potlucks, going to church, and attending Bible studies and retreats, all with believers. When we chose Lithia Park in Ashland, Oregon, as the place we would bring our Bride, and Easter Sunday as the day we would present her, I was scared to death.

We would be surrounded by all these people I hadn't paid attention to in many years. There would be a lot of non-believers. It made me feel like little David facing Goliath. I thought, *what have I gotten myself into?*

It was a lot scarier than I could have ever imagined. Thinking about it caused a wave of dread to fall over me until I was sick to my stomach. This was where the rubber would hit the road.

I should also mention that I was a huge chicken. I had never been stretched or pushed in any direction for an extended period. For years, I was happy to sit in the pew and study the Bible. I was perfectly pleased to see the pastor do all the work of leading people to Christ. As time passed, I had little contact with the outside world. The church consumed me, and I was happy to study and sit year after year. Of course, I would clap when our pastor would lead someone to Christ, and I was glad he was doing his job.

This time, I had a job to do, and it terrified me.

Easter Sunday arrived, the day we would take our Bride into the park following our church service. I woke, feeling dread, thinking, *Oh my goodness, what am I doing?* I would be bringing all those innocent people into some crazy idea from what I saw in a vision. If it all went south, it was all my fault.

The more I thought about it, the sicker I felt, until I finally lost my breakfast. I told myself that all I had to do was make it until 5:00 p.m. Then the whole crazy thing would be over.

In the Park

Following Easter service, my family grabbed Melissa, and we all piled into the car and went to a dear friend's house so Melissa could change into the wedding dress. Everyone thought I was fine, but I was dying inside. My kids were happy, and they seemed to be enjoying this new adventure, so I just bit my lip and took a deep breath. Then we were off to the park to do who knows what!

Once we arrived, I was surprised at how few people were in the park. Perhaps it was because it was Easter Sunday. I'm not sure, but I faithfully walked next to our beautiful Bride.

"This is going to be a lovely day, Melissa," I said. I knew I was lying through my teeth. I truly felt I was leading the lamb to the slaughter. *Oh God, help us*, I prayed. *What are we doing?*

She nodded with a beautiful smile lighting up her face. As we reached the park center, I adjusted her train, and we all stepped back, just like I saw in the vision. Then we left her standing there completely alone.

"Okay, God," I whispered. "What are you going to do? Please show up!"

Everything was set, just like in my vision, but the people were missing.

Then, to my surprise, which shouldn't have been a surprise at all, people began strolling on the pathway, gradually coming closer to where the Bride was standing. Soon, a steady stream of people came up to her.

"You're a beautiful bride," most said. "Are you about to get married?"

"Yes. I am about to be married." Her compelling voice drew people in. "And I am here on my Bridegroom's behalf. For you see, I have invited all my loved ones and special friends to be a part of this special day. And now you are on my Bridegroom's list."

Meanwhile, I was supposed to be saying something similar as I handed out invitations from a basket. I had a whole basket of little scrolls held together with gold rings. As I handed them to people, I could only get out one word.

"Here," I said as I stuffed the invitations into their hands.

I remember thinking that maybe someday, God would add more words to my vocabulary. Perhaps I could say, "Here's this."

Yet, despite my shortened vocabulary, we could all see that God was truly in charge. Everyone seemed intrigued and eager to take a scroll and unroll and read them. We will probably never know until we get to Heaven what kind of harvest that day produced, but the seeds of the vision were sown! Something marvelous was happening before our eyes.

Changing Lives for Eternity

Later, the confirmation of this moment came clearly through the reading of the parable of the wedding Feast in Matthew 22:1-10:

> *And Jesus answered and spoke to them again by parables and said: "The kingdom of heaven is like a certain king who arranged a marriage for his son, and sent out his servants to call those who were invited to the wedding; and they were not willing to come.*
>
> *Again, he sent out other servants, saying, "Tell those who are invited, 'See, I have prepared my dinner; my oxen and fatted cattle are killed, and all things are ready. Come to the wedding.'"*

*But they made light of it and went their ways, one to
his own farm, another to his business. And the rest
seized his servants, treated them spitefully,
and killed them.
But when the king heard about it, he was furious.
And he sent out his armies, destroyed those
murderers, and burned up their city.
Then he said to his servants, "The wedding
is ready, but those who were invited were
not worthy. Therefore go into the highways, and as
many as you find, invite to the wedding."*

*So those servants went out into the highways
and gathered together all whom they found,
both bad and good.
And the wedding hall was filled with guests.*

I love how Jesus says in this passage of Scripture to invite the bad and the good. I also love how he puts the bad before the good.

In retrospect, I now understand a lot more than I did in the beginning. God was definitely calling us to show people a vision of what it was like to be forgiven and loved by Him. The purity, the beauty, and the humility of the Bride of Christ are irresistible.

A future bride has lots of goals to accomplish before the day of her wedding. One duty that belongs to her is sending out invitations and putting together a guest list. It's her job to invite all her friends and family but also to invite the groom's friends and family. Everyone must receive that special invitation, so they know they're invited and so they won't miss that special day.

One of the things I loved hearing Melissa say as the Bride of Christ is, "Yes, I am about to be married, and I am here on my Bridegroom's behalf. For you see, I have invited all my loved ones and special friends to be a part of this special day. And now you are on my Bridegroom's list."

Dear friend, I don't know you personally, but God does, and He loves you dearly, and He does not want you to miss His coming. He does not want you to miss this special day that will change your life for eternity. You are invited today to come and receive Christ as your Bridegroom.

That first day was almost like a birth. With all the emotion beforehand . . . my worrying that I brought all those innocent people to be a part of something I still didn't understand; then seeing with my own eyes a miracle as God's favor fell on the Bride . . . it truly was the birth of my vision. The Bride was outside the church walls in all her glory, pouring out God's love to a lost world.

For me, I had no words for the lost as I could only get out the word "Here" as I handed out invitations. I had been in the church so long I had lost my ability to speak to non-believers. I'm pretty sure that was the same for most of us that day. We were taking baby steps in evangelism. Taking one step is the beginning of winning the battle over the fear of man.

4

The Vision Goes to the Streets

Getting Attention

THE PEAR BLOSSOM is a local annual spring parade we celebrate every year in my town. It was only a few weeks away, and I was still living off the joy of the wonderful day we had with our Bride in the park.

My husband Clyde said, "I think we should build a float and enter the Pear Blossom Parade."

I stared at him. Surely, he was kidding. I had barely made it through the park scene, and now he wanted to do a parade? And what about building a float? We had never attempted such a thing. Then I heard myself say, "Well, we do have a trailer... but what about a truck?"

Clyde didn't miss a beat. "We can borrow one."

I learned something significant about that season of our lives. There are three times in life when you can get somebody's attention—birth, death, and a parade!

The exciting part was we had truly bitten off more than we could chew, so we needed help, and lots of it. Dozens of wonderful believers came alongside and helped us with all the great ideas of how to make this the most beautiful float anyone had ever seen.

Our church had a worship meeting every Friday night. After the service, we would all pile into the church coffee shop for fellowship. Clyde and I would bring our invitations and the gold rings and set them on the table. Then everyone there would grab a bunch of each and start to roll them up. It was on these special nights when we truly became "Holy Rollers."

Thousands of our invitations got rolled on those Friday nights to be used in our future outreaches. Many of the people who helped us, and others from our church who heard what we were doing, ended up volunteering to help us put together our floats and hand out invitations at the parades. Some of their daughters became little flower girls on the floats.

We created a beautiful floral arch on the float and set a huge table representing the wedding Feast before the Bride. We placed banners along the float so people could understand who we were and what we were about. The front banner said, "Spirit and the Bride say Come!" in beautiful sparkling gold, while the back banner said, "Come Just As You Are."

The little flower girls, dressed in colorful dresses, sat all along the sides of the float. They were incredibly adorable and experienced the thrill of their lives being a part of this beautiful float. Our Bride stood beneath the canopy in all her glory.

A group of us walked beside the float while carrying huge baskets full of rolled invitations inviting everyone to the Bride's glorious wedding in Heaven. We inflated hundreds of white helium balloons with "The Hope of Heaven" written in gold letters. Dozens of volunteers handed them out.

Many small Oregon towns have local parades for different events or holidays. To our delight, we found such favor in these parades that we won first place repeatedly. We traveled six-and-a-half hours from our home in Southern Oregon all the way up to John Day, a small town in Eastern Oregon about 189 miles from Boise, Idaho. Then we traveled to the Oregon coast, entering all the local parades in every city. We participated in at least forty-one parades.

Taking part in those parades was one of the happiest times of my life to see our family and precious servants of God traveling together and working hand-in-hand to reach the lost for Christ.

One time, as we were putting the finishing touches on the float minutes before the parade was about to start, a couple came up to us and asked if we were Jehovah's Witnesses.

We told them, "No, we are not."

Then they said, "Oh, then you must be Mormons."

I said, "No, we are Christians."

The girl was a bit shocked and said, "We didn't know Christians shared their faith publicly!"

I responded, "Well, we do now!"

Seconds later, our float was moving down the street.

While we were in the town of John Day, I told God I was feeling anxious and awkward about talking to strangers.

He said to me, "They aren't strangers to Me. I died for every single face you will see today. Those faces were before me when I was on the cross."

Suddenly, I saw His amazing compassion for the lost. My fear of man was taken away. Since that day, I have never met a stranger.

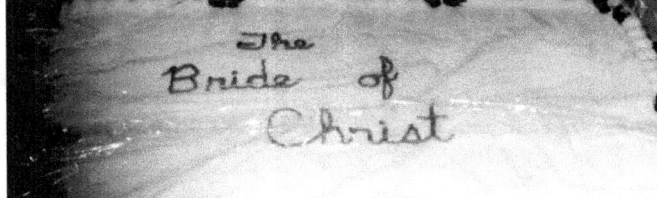

Part 2
The Bride's Invitation

5

The Bride Comes out of the Closet

Looking for the Lost Sheep

> *... Let the bridegroom*
> *go forth of his chamber,*
> *and the bride out of her closet.*
> —Joel 2:16 (KJV)

I LOVE THE VERSE referring to letting the Bride out of the closet. Everyone else is out. I think it's our turn.

After one of our parades, I saw one of our helpers walk boldly into a bar with a basket of bridal invitations. My first thought was, *Oh! Can we do that?*

I hadn't been in a bar for years and had pretty much ignored their existence. So out of curiosity, I followed her. There she was with her basket of invitations and was happily handing them out to everyone sitting at the bar.

How intriguing.

People willingly took the invitations and immediately began reading them.

Seeing their response opened a whole new door. The invitations seemed to hold a special kind of intrigue. I watched people's faces. Everyone wanted to receive an invitation. I watched as people read them, and I began to see that we were reaching a deeper need within many of them. It was like seeing the sun shining amid dark clouds. I could almost feel the warmth from the Son. It was like the parable of the lost sheep in Luke 15:4. "What man of you, having a hundred sheep, if he loses one of them, does not leave the ninety-nine in the wilderness, and go after the one which is lost until he finds it?"

Just like the shepherd who began earnestly looking for that one lost sheep, we, too, found ourselves taking baby steps into seriously looking for the lost. This time we did not use the bridal theme or attire. We were simply servants, one beggar telling another beggar where the bread was. We were now used to talking with strangers, which alleviated one massive obstacle for me. As my evangelism was growing, I also realized I was losing all fear and speaking boldly in love with strangers about my Savior.

A New Invitation

Since we didn't have the float to help explain who we were, we came up with a new invitation in the form of a poem called "The Rose."

> This Rose is very special, it's made with you in mind.
> It's from someone who loves you and is with you all the time.
> Although you cannot see Him, He is always very near.
> He longs to give you peace and cast out all your fear.
> It's never hard to find Him, just open up your heart.
> Then nothing ever again can keep you two apart.
> He gave His life for yours when He died upon the cross.
> This made a bridge to Heaven that you can now cross.
> He rose from the dead so He could be with you.
> Now you decide, my precious, do you long for His love too?
> Ask Him to forgive you for all that you have done.
> Tell Him you believe that Jesus is His son,
> And that God came to earth in the form of a man,
> And to show you that He loves you, He died and rose again.
> Now, if you said this prayer and believe with all your heart,
> You and Jesus are now one. Enjoy your brand-new start.

We rolled the poem into a scroll, like we did with our bridal invitations, and closed each one with a gold band. We were used to being surrounded by flowers during our float days, so I thought it would be great to hand out small bouquets with the Rose invitations stuffed inside.

But where were we going to get hundreds and hundreds of beautiful flowers? We had zero budget to speak of, which I have now repeatedly discovered is an excellent place to see God's fun begin.

I called Albertsons and spoke to the florist. She offered me seven roses that I could pick up. "Well, that's a good start Lord," I prayed, "but I was hoping for a lot more."

Still, it was a start, so I drove down to pick them up. I walked in, looking for the black bucket the florist had set aside for me. I couldn't find it anywhere, but what I did see were bunches and bunches of all kinds of flowers in the trash can. That certainly made me wonder. *What are they going to do with those?*

I finally found the florist to ask about the black bucket.

"I'm sorry," she said. "I don't believe we have ever spoken. Perhaps you are at the wrong Albertsons."

Suddenly, I realized she was right. "Oh my goodness! This is embarrassing, but since I'm here, can I ask you something?"

"Sure," she said.

"What are you going to do with all those flowers in the trash can?"

"Oh," she said. "Those flowers are outdated, so we can't sell them even though they're still good. It's like with everything in the grocery store. Once they have reached their expiration date, they can no longer be sold."

I took in a deep breath, "Really?" My next words came out in a rush as I told her what I hoped to do in reaching the lost for

Christ. To my surprise, she got it! She gave me permission to take not only those flowers, but to come by every Friday, and she would set aside all the dated flowers for me.

"And I'll keep them in water," she said, "instead of throwing them in the trash can."

"Praise God!" I said, meaning it. No other words would come out. God had done far more than I could have ever dreamed. We now had all kinds of beautiful flowers to make our wonderfully gorgeous bouquets.

Into the Bars

My friend Crystal and I got together every Friday and Saturday night and made hundreds of beautiful bouquets wrapped in cellophane with the Rose invitation tucked safely inside. Crystal and I filled an enormous wicker basket with our beautiful bouquets, and Clyde drove us to town and chaperoned us as we walked into bar after bar.

We would sweetly walk to each table and offer the girls one of our beautiful bouquets. Often people would want to pay for them as they were so beautiful. Always, when I saw a guy and girl sitting together, I would say to the guy, "Wouldn't you love to give your sweet girl a beautiful bouquet?"

"Of course," he would invariably say and often offered to pay.

But we said, "Oh, no. We're so happy to do this."

We were always thinking of the beautiful poem hidden inside, praying with all hope that the Lord would someday touch the woman's heart.

One time, as we were walking from table to table, I saw a man looking at me with a huge smirk on his face. When I got closer, he said in a thunderous voice, "I suppose you're going to tell me I'm a sinner, and I'm going to hell, right?"

"Oh, no!" I said, "I'm here to tell you that you are one hundred percent loved by God."

He nearly fell off his stool!

Disagreement

Not everyone in our church agreed with our new path into the bars. It soon became the topic of an elders meeting. Some of the elders were quite excited about what we were doing, but my pastor was not happy about our new direction.

"I'm worried," he said, "that you are encouraging others to follow in your footsteps, but some of them may be tempted to fall back into their old way of living."

I could see his point, but I also knew in my heart that God had called us to this very thing. "I'm not inviting anyone to join us," I said. "Sometimes things just have to play themselves out."

He shook his head. "I can't support you in this, Debbie."

"Okay," I said. "Let's say in ten years you walk by a bar, and as you're looking in the window, you see me in a drunken stupor on the floor, then you win. But if in ten years you see people free from this bondage, I win."

"Fair enough," he said. "Let's see what happens."

So many times, I wished he could have been with me at the end of the night as I watched girls walking in every direction proudly holding their beautiful bouquets. It was surely a sight to behold. My heart soared. I felt God was saying, "Job well done, good and faithful servants."

Let them do good,
That they may be rich in good works,
ready to give, willing to share,
storing up for themselves a good foundation
for the time to come,
that they may lay hold on eternal life.
—1 Timothy 6:18-19

6

The Bride Goes into the Darkness

A Very Dark Hole

ONE AFTERNOON, I WAS VISITING my friend Carol who owned a flower shop, when a group of women arrived. One of the ladies was a future Bride coming to pick out her wedding bouquet. I did not know her personally, but she recognized me and knew about my new adventure in handing out flowers in bars.

She took my hand into hers and said, "I know what you're doing. Please come to my wedding." Then she burst into tears. "And afterward, I want you to take my rose bouquet into the strip club."

Her tears were falling hard now. "Debbie, I want you to give my roses to the girls working there."

By the time she finished, the entire group of women, including myself, were weeping. It was a moment I will never forget. I knew God was doing something above and beyond what I could ever think or plan. I had never thought about entering a strip club. It seemed like such a dark hole, and it was easier to pretend it didn't exist. Now I felt God had commissioned to enter that very place. I was relieved when Carol told me in tears that she would go with me. This was a God appointment for her as well.

On the day of her wedding, the bride gave me her bouquet of twenty-four pink roses. I brought the bouquet back to Carol's shop, where we made twenty-four separate bouquets out of the roses with the bridal invitation tucked neatly inside.

It was around 10:00 p.m. that night when we arrived at the club. Clyde was our driver, and the three of us sat in the car earnestly praying for a very long time. I had dressed in the wedding gown for this special occasion. My dress was so full I barely fit in the car, and then I could barely move. I'm not sure I would have ever gotten out of the car if Clyde hadn't finally opened the door for us.

"I'll be waiting in the car," Clyde said, "and I'll be praying."

I will never forget walking into that black hole.

A young woman was at the desk, so I handed her the first bouquet. Her face turned ashen as if she had seen a ghost. I didn't realize until later that the desk was where we were supposed to pay to enter. All we did was smile and walk right in.

Black lights lit the room, so I was glowing white when the lights caught my dress. I expected to see women with bare breasts, but to my surprise, most had no clothes on at all. I walked around, handing every woman who worked there a beautiful rose bouquet. Each encounter was very sweet, and I will never forget how the women gently held their bouquets with such care. It was as if they were holding a newborn baby.

As walked around the room, I stumbled into a small dark room off the main stage. A man was sitting on a chair with his back to me, and a woman was sitting on his lap. I was sure he would want to give her a rose, so I gingerly tapped him on the shoulder. I'll never forget how his head whipped around and seeing his eyes as big as saucers.

I said, "Excuse me but wouldn't you love to give the beautiful girl a rose?"

He never said a word, but he took the rose and gave it to her.

I remember thinking how easy it was to interrupt sin, as long as the interruption was done in love. At that point, I found Carol again, and we had both finished handing out all twenty-four rose bouquets. We said our goodbyes, smiling at the young woman at the front desk, and then we left.

When we got into the car, we relayed our story to Clyde. We could hardly believe what had just happened. All we knew at the time was something beyond ourselves had taken place in the midst of darkness.

Beginning to Question

As the days turned into months, however, I began to question what we were doing. Were we truly making any difference?

"God," I prayed, "If I could know of just one girl who has placed her hope in you, then all my doubts will be erased."

Do you ever wonder if God hears your prayers? Well, He must have heard mine, because soon after that prayer, I received a letter. It wasn't just any letter. It was a special letter sent to me from a great man of God I highly admired, and it spoke of several women whose lives were changed because of our visit to the strip club.

Dear Debbie,

I want to share something wonderful with you.

Two months ago, I met a young couple at Ashland Christian Fellowship who told me they had been living in the pit of hell and really wanted to get right with God. They lived together for five years, were heavily into drugs and had two young daughters out of wedlock. Well, to make a long story short, last Saturday, June 29, I married this couple in a beautiful Christian ceremony, and yesterday, I dedicated their children to the Lord and then baptized the couple in the creek behind the fellowship.

Over breakfast, this young lady confessed to me that only a few months ago, she was a stripper. She went on to describe the odd appearance of a lovely woman who came into her club, dressed as a bride, and gave her a flower with a note inside that said, "Jesus loves you." She told me that this simple act filled her with shame at her lifestyle, and that she and two other strippers ended up weeping together. It was that night she decided she had to change her life.

The rest is all God.

Today, this young woman is a new creation in Christ, a happily married Christian bride and mother, and has a joy and a glow that are unmistakably our Lord and Savior's. What a miracle!

Often, we don't get to see the fruit produced by the seeds we scatter. And so I'm blessed to be able to share with you the impact that your Bride of Christ Ministry is having. And may I encourage you to keep reaching out to those lost and lonely souls. Every stripper is someone's abused and abandoned daughter, and all of them, whether or not they know, are longing for the love of Jesus Christ. Thank you for having the courage to do what you do.

>	Your brother in Christ,
>	love,
>	PK Hallinan

Out of Darkness

I learned from that experience that I was witnessing to people sitting in darkness. It was so dark that even if someone wanted to leave, they could not find the door. I believe that during that particular night, Carol and I brought in the least bit of light. If the slightest bit of light can enter these dark holes, the ones whom God is calling will truly be able to get up and find the door. How can we not bring the light into those dark places?

> *He brought them out of darkness*
> *and the shadow of death,*
> *And broke their chains in pieces.*
> *Oh, that* men *would give thanks to the LORD*
> *for His goodness,*
> *And for His wonderful works to the children of men!*
> *For He has broken the gates of bronze,*
> *And cut the bars of iron in two.*
> —*Psalm 107:14-16*

7

The Bride Seeks the Lost

Seeking the Lost

MY ONE VISIT TO THE STRIP CLUB opened a whole new understanding of Luke 19:10. *"for the Son of Man has come to seek and to save that which was lost."* For the first time, I was beginning to realize the depth in which Jesus was willing to go and the primary purpose for His calling.

To get a better understanding, I looked up the word "lost" in the dictionary. The first words were pretty self-explanatory: "missing, mislaid, misplaced, vanished, strayed, stray, absent." But then the words took a turn for the worse: "destroyed, wrecked, demolished, ruined, wiped out, eradicated, extirpated, killed, murdered and perished."

I had to wonder at these words. They certainly placed a much deeper meaning than just simply the word lost. And I never equated the word "lost" with the death sentence.

Then I looked up the word "seek." That search painted a much deeper picture for me. The true meanings for "seek" were: "try to find, search for, look for, track down, look into, dig for, probe for, investigate, explore, examine, scrutinize, inspect, nose out, sniff out, scout out, trace, pursue, be after, and go in for."

Now that was the one that got me: "go in for." For the first time, I began to have a clear picture of why Jesus would leave the ninety-nine for that one lost sheep. He knew that a sheep would die if somebody didn't find it.

> *What man of you, having a hundred sheep,*
> *if he loses one of them,*
> *does not leave the ninety-nine in the wilderness,*
> *and go after the one which is lost until he finds it?*
> —Luke 15:4

Seeking the One

In all my years of Bible study, I never realized Jesus wanted us to partner with Him in searching for that lost one. I had always thought the lost somehow found their way to church, and it was the pastor's job to lead them to Christ at the end of the service. Plain and simple. No hunting, no searching, they just showed up.

Now, for the first time, I realized not all lost sheep come in on their own. In fact, according to Scripture, you usually have to go get them wherever they are. All these new revelations prompted me to go back into the club. But perhaps my primary motivation was to get a taste of the love of God—such amazing love that He was willing to leave the ninety-nine and go in search of that lost one, no matter where it was.

So, I returned every week.

I tried to be inconspicuous by dressing in street clothes rather than a wedding gown. Once inside, I searched madly for the dressing room. I hoped to give the young women more flowers and personally get to know them.

My beginning visits didn't work out very well. The club was pitch black, and I was usually escorted out before finding dressing room. On one of my returns, I found it. It was right next to the sound booth. As I reached for the doorknob, I couldn't help but notice somebody had kicked the door really hard, because their foot left a big hole in the bottom of the door.

Once inside, I discovered the bathroom stalls had no doors. I thought, *Oh my gosh, they are given no privacy at all.* I had no sooner placed my beautiful bouquet on the countertop when the bouncer charged in after me. He grabbed me roughly by my arm without saying a word and quickly led me out of the building, where he began to warn me that I was never to come back in *or else.*

Now, that was a problem, because Easter was four weeks away, and my friends and I had been putting together Easter baskets for all the girls. My friend Kim and I had gotten the word out, and everyone we knew had pitched in to fill the baskets with wonderful goodies. The baskets were absolutely beautiful. We had stuffed them with everything possible, from skincare products to perfume and all kinds of Easter candy. Each of the twenty-five baskets had a New Testament tucked sweetly inside, and each was wrapped in colored cellophane with an enormous, beautiful bow on top.

Now, what was I going to do?

Big Chicken

I could tell the bouncer was terribly mad at me, and I was afraid of him. So, I did the only thing I could think of at the time. I rented a whole rabbit costume complete with a giant rabbit head. No way would he recognize me in that getup.

The night before I planned to deliver the baskets in the rabbit costume, my church showed the film, "The Passion of Christ," by Mel Gibson. Upon seeing the vivid truth of how Jesus was tortured and how greatly He suffered on our behalf, I was deeply touched.

I began to feel ashamed that I had rented the rabbit costume. Was I too afraid to stand up and admit I was a Christian? Could I not handle even a tiny bit of persecution?

You're a big chicken. You should have rented a chicken outfit.

Despite the bouncer's warning, I decided to deliver the baskets as me. I determined I would not regard my safety no matter what might happen to me.

I made many trips into the club, because I couldn't carry all the baskets at the same time. I kept looking for the bouncer but, strangely, I never saw him anywhere. I found out later that one of the girls had her jaw broken the night before, and the bouncer was out in hot pursuit of the guy who did it.

From then on, it was pretty smooth sailing.

I soon learned that the employees at these places shift quickly, and the old bouncer who hated me apparently moved on. I decided to try and befriend the new bouncer with gifts. Every time I came in, I brought him a bag of beef jerky. At Christmas, I had no trouble dropping off small live Christmas trees from Harry and David in the dressing room.

On Valentine's Day, I brought in beautiful red helium balloons that said in a beautiful font, "Jesus Loves You and Wants You in Heaven." One time as I was walking in with quite a few balloons, it was so dark I couldn't see a thing. The balloons got caught in the overhead ceiling fan. That was definitely a bit of a disruption.

Fortunately, most people thought it was quite funny!

We never missed one holiday from Christmas to Mother's Day. These lovely ladies were constantly reminded how much they were loved and wanted by God.

One night as I was approaching the club, I saw a girl working an outdoor food stand directly across the street. She spotted me and waved me over.

"I used to be one of the dancers at the club, "she said. Then she began to tell me how every time she got a Rose poem in her flower bouquet, she would tape it to her wall at home. "I asked Jesus into my heart, and now I have no desire to live that lifestyle again."

I heard many stories through the years of girls who once danced at the strip club and are now free to love God and be the women He always promised they could be.

People often ask me how they can know they are following God. I think one of the best ways is NOT to know where He's taking you but to follow anyway.

If anyone serves Me,
Let him follow Me;
And where I am,
There My servant will be also.
If anyone serves Me,
him My Father will honor.
—John 12:26

8

The Bride Takes Part in Halloween Night

Harvest Party

HALLOWEEN NIGHT WAS APPROACHING. I had this flash of a thought, wondering if someone could get saved on such a horrid night. In my Christian experience, I only thought of Halloween as strictly the devil's night and something Christians should denounce completely. We stayed in our Churches on those nights and left the devil alone.

Still curious about whether someone could get saved despite all the evil, I called Ashland Christian Fellowship and spoke with a pastor. He had quite a story to tell.

"Thousands of people, fill the plaza on Halloween night," he said. "They wear costumes and drink and do drugs and walk around all night celebrating. I know, because I used to be one of them."

I sat back in my chair, astonished.

He went on to tell me how he had once been so stoned he could no longer stand up. He was lying halfway on the street when a little girl walked past him and simply said, "Jesus loves you."

Those simple words would not leave his head.

Somehow, though he didn't remember how, he made it home. And still, those words, "Jesus loves you," haunted him. He heard them being said over and over in his head. They wouldn't stop. The next day, out of total frustration, he went into Ashland Christian Fellowship.

"Make the words stop!" he pleaded. The pastors discovered demons had long tormented him. On that day, he received deliverance and asked Jesus to be his Lord and Savior.

"My answer to you, Debbie," he said, "is a big 'Yes!' Halloween night is a real harvest party in the true sense of the word. How else could you get thousands of people who don't know Jesus all standing in the same place?"

Into the Night

So, Clyde and I went into the dark night, me in my wedding gown, believing God directed us to go and invite the bad and the good to the wedding in Heaven.

There I stood with my huge basket of candy and rolled invitations inviting everyone to my wedding.

The Bride Takes Part in Halloween Night

Ashland is a great theater town, so the costumes were unbelievably authentic. Every type of costume you could imagine was there in full glory that night. I was passing out my invitations when I suddenly came face-to-face with the devil! Real horns seemed to protrude out of his forehead.

As he approached, he looked me in the eyes and calmly said, "I know who you are."

"Oh, you do? Who am I?"

"You are the Bride of Christ."

I took a small step back, "How do you know?"

"I'm the devil," he said. "I know these things." And then he turned and was gone.

Needless to say, he didn't receive an invitation.

The meeting with the devil shook me, he seemed so real, but we continued passing out invitations and helium balloons. I had thought the balloons with our "Hope of Heaven" written in gold on them would be a nice gesture. But it wasn't long before we saw our mistake. People who received the balloons were more interested in the helium inside. We laughed and made a note of no balloons next year.

The Axe Swinger

The following Halloween, we showed up again. It was my second time, so I felt freer to walk outside the main circle of town toward people on the outskirts near the park. I came across a man who looked like a woodsman carrying an enormous hatchet. Black make-up circled his eyes, giving him a very foreboding look.

I happily handed him an invitation, which he nearly grabbed out of my hand before ripping it into pieces. As I watched the pieces fall to the ground, he began screaming at me with such force that spit drooled from his mouth. He was spewing the most horrible swear words.

I just stood there in shock.

No way was I the least bit prepared for his outburst. Last year's event went so smoothly. Even the devil was cordial. In the midst of the man's spitting and profanity, I tried my best to reason with him.

Big mistake.

"What have I done to make you so angry?" I asked.

"You completely ruined our Halloween last year!" he shouted.

I was shocked at his words, "How did I do that?"

"You just ruined it!" Your very presence ruined it!" Then he added more horrible words that seemed to make him angrier. "You need to stay in church where you belong!"

I was trying to process what he was saying and also thinking I needed to move on, but my legs wouldn't move. He had screamed so loud that he had drawn a crowd. People surrounded us, and I was pretty much hemmed in.

That's when the man began to swing the hatchet.

The Bride Takes Part in Halloween Night

It hit the pavement with brute force as he swung at bits of the invitation. Sparks were flying off the blade. I could hardly take in a breath as I watched him swing the hatchet over and over.

I called out to God with one word, "Help!"

I'll never forget how I heard God speak.

God said very clearly, "Put out your hand."

"No!" I said aloud. "He'll chop it off!"

Again, I heard God tell me to put out my hand.

So, I put out my hand, right in the middle of one of the man's swings of the hatchet. I'm pretty sure my eyes were closed.

To my great surprise, the man dropped the hatchet and grabbed my hand.

I instantly knew I had heard God correctly. "What's your name?"

"Ned. My name is Ned."

I held his hands tightly and said, "God loves you, Ned."

It seemed he was very near tears now. "How do you know! How do you know!"

I kept my voice soft. "Because He's telling me right now. He loves you."

I let go of his hand and, as the crowd parted, I walked away.

God had wanted to speak to Ned, and He did, through me.

I never saw Ned for the rest of the night, but I remember keeping an eye out so I wouldn't be caught off guard, just in case. In fact, I never saw Ned again, even on the following year's Halloween night. I hope he's pastoring a church somewhere, because I know without a shadow of a doubt, God touched Ned on that Halloween night.

Beauty of the Second Mile

The lesson I learned from that experience is the beauty of the second mile. People are dying to see Christ, but often He's not visible in the first mile, so that's why Jesus says when someone asks you to go one mile, go the second.

My first mile with Ned was when I stood still while he ranted and raged, yet he did not see Jesus. My second mile was when I reached out my hand. It was then God showed Himself. I believe God touched Ned and that somehow, somewhere, he is a changed man, simply because of the love of God.

> *And whoever compels you to go one mile,*
> *go with him two.*
> —Matthew 5:41

Part 3
The Bride's Journey

9

Into All the World

A Real Evangelist

> *And He said to them,*
> *"Go into all the world and preach*
> *the gospel to every creature."*
> *—Mark 16:15*

THE BRIDE MINISTRY took us on a journey I would have never dreamed of and to places and countries I would have never thought I would be able to go. Places like Amsterdam. When I reflect on Amsterdam, the Scripture that comes to mind is Matthew 23:37 about how often God has longed to gather His children together as a hen gathers her chicks under her wings, but His children were not willing.

> *Jerusalem, Jerusalem, you who kill*
> *the prophets and stone those sent to you,*
> *how often I have longed to gather*

> *your children together,*
> *as a hen gathers her chicks under her wings,*
> *and you were not willing.*
> —Matthew 23:37 (NIV)

When Jesus said to go into the world and preach the gospel, I never thought he could possibly be speaking to me. After all, it was hard enough to take the gospel into our local park. Amsterdam wasn't even a thought in my mind.

Then one day, our church announced Billy Graham was having an annual outreach to evangelists in a huge convention hall in Amsterdam. Graham had a burden for evangelists that prompted this event. All kinds of schools and training for pastors and teachers were available, but little was offered to train up an evangelist. Because of this, Graham would hold special conventions calling evangelists from all around the world to come and be trained and encouraged. He would feature one of the top evangelists of our day, such as Luis Palau, Joni Eareckson Tada, or Greg Laurie. Graham hoped that with the help of good training, evangelism would get a shot in the arm.

Clyde and I were excited. We were evangelists. We were doing our best to get the gospel out to the masses. We could sure use the training, but there was a massive obstacle in front of us. Graham only invited ten thousand people to these special meetings. Considering people came from all over the world, it seemed unlikely we could be part of that ten thousand.

Still, we excitedly filled out the paperwork, explaining how we were reaching the lost as the Bride of Christ. To our surprise, we received the invitation in a few short weeks. We felt privileged to have been invited to Amsterdam; Lithia Park seemed a far cry in Ashland, Oregon.

For the first time, I felt we were true evangelists. No longer did I have to fight the fear of man. I was willing and excited to embrace this new unique calling. But I'm ashamed of what happened soon after.

A Woman in Pain

A few days before the trip, I was in the Dollar Store looking for a journal, because I certainly wanted to document everything I was hoping to see. While I was looking at the journals, a woman came up to me.

"I have a toothache," she said.

"I'm sorry."

I reached past her and picked up one of the journals before hurrying to the next aisle. To my surprise, she popped up in front of me again.

"I'm hurting," she said. "I'm in pain."

"I'm so sorry," I said, but in my mind, I thought, *I'm getting ready to go to Amsterdam. I don't have time for anything else.* I turned and hurried out of the store.

It wasn't until later, on the fourteen-hour plane ride, that God gently got my attention and brought up the woman in the Dollar

Store. I realized then that what I thought was an inconvenience was actually a divine appointment.

I sat back in my seat, ashamed.

How much of the ministry of Jesus happened on the *way* to where He was going? It wasn't just about reaching His destination. In fact, most of His ministry appeared to be almost by chance. I realized for the first time that what happens along the journey is just as important as reaching the destination.

I thought about the woman. What if I had stopped and prayed for her? Was God's plan to heal her? I would never know, because I hadn't taken the time to reach out to her.

"I'm sorry, God," I whispered. "I'll try to do better next time."

And then I prayed for the woman, that God would send someone else her way who would take time to help.

I learned through that experience that divine appointments are good at wearing disguises, and I determined to do my best to recognize them and allow God to use me along the way.

10

Bridal Love

Understanding the Bride of Christ

AS TIME WENT ON in our ministry, I started having my own personal revelation about the Bride of Christ. In the early days of my newfound faith, I had learned that Christ had accepted me as a child of God. But accepting love from my Bridegroom Jesus was a process for me. When I first envisioned the beautiful Bride in the park, I was not looking at an image of myself. It was someone else entirely. I saw someone beautiful, something I didn't see in myself.

Growing up, I had severe buck teeth, which didn't bother my parents, so I figured it was something I had to live with. I tried using humor as my defense. I would make fun of myself by always laughing with my hand over my mouth.

It wasn't until I was twenty-eight years old that I finally took matters into my own hands and was fitted with braces. Four teeth had to be pulled to push my two front teeth into their proper place. It has always been difficult for me to shake the image of that buck-toothed little girl I used to be. The only compliment I remember receiving in my youth was from a teacher who told me I had a nice speaking voice.

That's why, as we progressed in our Bride ministry, I was happy to be the Bride's helper. I was honored to walk alongside her, support her, and pray for her. I watched in wonder as I witnessed God pour His love and favor upon her during all our parades. Then one day, it all changed.

I wasn't looking for more; I was genuinely content being a servant. Then, in one of my devotional times, it seemed like God spoke out of the blue and said, "Who is my Bride?"

My first thought was, *What? Why are you asking me this?*

Silence fell over the room, and I felt like God's eyes were directly on me. I became very uncomfortable. Then I heard myself say, "Don't look at me!"

I didn't feel worthy. I was too imperfect to be loved in that manner. I had my legitimate reasons, just like the Shulamite woman in the Song of Solomon. I echoed her words as she said:

> *Do not look upon me, because I am dark,*
> *Because the sun has tanned me . . .*
> —*Song of Solomon 1:6*

In her own eyes, she was lacking. She goes on to say that her mother's sons were angry with her. Her own family, who was supposed to love her the most, didn't give her the confidence, love and support she needed. They took advantage of her, and their demand for her hard labor was so exhaustive that she couldn't keep her own vineyard.

I felt as if she was speaking for me because of my words and reasoning, because I lacked the faith to accept bridal love. She knew how that felt.

I imagined the Bridegroom patiently listening to all the pain she had to share. It was then his turn to speak to her in his love language. He explained how he saw her.

> *I have compared you, my love,*
> *To my filly among Pharaoh's chariots.*
> *Your cheeks are lovely with ornaments,*
> *Your neck with chains of gold . . .*
> *. . . . Behold you are fair, my love!*
> *Behold you are fair! You have dove's eyes.*
> —Song of Solomon 1:9-10 and 15

I sat in awe as this revelation came to me. I learned that unless I were willing to see myself through the eyes of the Bridegroom, I would never feel worthy of that kind of love.

Weeping now, I whispered, "Yes. I will be your Bride."

That moment is hard to put into words. I died to my lack of self-worth and surrendered to God's love. It was painful and beautiful at the same time. I knew He had changed me, and I was willing to accept His love.

"Yes," I said. "Yes! I will be your Bride."

11

Amsterdam

Ten Thousand Evangelists

AS I WAS PRAYING about this new leap of faith, I kept thinking about Amsterdam's famous Red Light District. I felt I had to see it for myself, but would we even be able to find it?

Clyde and I prayed that we would be able to find it and that God would do something extraordinary. We both felt strongly I was supposed to go there.

When we arrived in Amsterdam, I was so tired from the long fourteen-hour flight that I barely remember getting off the plane. My legs were swollen from the long plane ride, and I wasn't even sure I could walk. A bus took us to the conference center to register.

When we reached the stadium, it was truly amazing to be in the presence of ten thousand evangelists from all over the world.

But the lines were tremendous, and my feet were swelling even worse.

Even through all the pain, I was amazed at Amsterdam's beauty. Flowers decorated the entire city. They were on balconies and sidewalks, and every corner had a flower stall. Bicycles were moving everywhere, and a canal was going right through the middle of it all. I had never seen such a beautiful city.

After a good rest, my legs worked for me again. No one had ever told me anything about Amsterdam. I felt as if someone had dropped me into the beginning of a fairy tale. Clyde and I had never had a honeymoon, but we were having one now. Everything was so very pretty. Our room featured beautiful white sheer linen curtains. I'll never forget those curtains. I now have sheer white curtains in my bedroom.

Once we got settled and learned our daily routine, we realized many participants were unsure of a specific calling or how to become successful evangelists. We, on the other hand, knew what God called us to do. We were anxious to go into the streets and invite people to the wedding. We had special wedding invitations printed in French, German, and Dutch.

After a few days, we began to wonder why more of the evangelists in training were not moving in that direction. After all, we were in Amsterdam, for Heaven's sake. If any place needed to hear the good news, it was here! Amsterdam is well known as one of the sin capitals of the world. Everywhere, we saw evidence of a free flow of alcohol, drugs, and prostitution.

We discovered that Billy Graham had cut everybody loose a few years before to go tell the good news. Ten thousand evangelists hit the streets! Unfortunately, it didn't go well. The methods many used to share their faith were not well received from the locals. Instead of a happy reception, quite a backlash happened. From that point on, Billy encouraged the evangelists in training to stay on campus. They spent their free time watching movies and being entertained instead of sharing the good news.

After learning this information, Clyde and I decided we would leave campus for a day and look at the downtown area for ourselves.

Breaking up the Party

The next day, we stumbled across the famous Red Light District. It was quite an attraction. Regular tour buses drove up and down the street so tourists could get a firsthand look at the depravity of man. I was in my street clothes at the time, and Clyde thought it was best that I walk down the street alone and report back as to what was possible for me to do.

I walked down the street, which was lined with small rooms almost like a window setting of a department store display. Each cubicle had one door with one woman standing or sitting on a stool facing the public. The women wore very little clothing, and most were revealing their breasts. It was an overwhelming sight to see. I was deeply saddened to see the level of depravity and sin on display for all to see.

Some of the windows had a curtain drawn across them, which meant a client was inside. I learned later that each cubicle came equipped with a single bed off to the side. I remember thinking, *Oh boy, this is bigger than I ever imagined. I'm in over my head.*

I ended up standing in front of a cubicle featuring a beautiful woman of color. A crowd of people stood around me. All I could think to do was point to Heaven and to my heart and pantomime how God loves her.

She took one look at me, then her face contorted with anger as she motioned for me to move out of the way.

I turned and saw that I was blocking the men behind me trying to view her. I moved away, nearly overcome with discouragement. It all seemed so impossible. Did these girls have any idea of what they were doing to themselves? Did some of them not have a way out?

Curious faces filled the streets, all there to view the girls, not for who they were, but for how the girl's bodies could satisfy a gnawing lust.

Returning to Clyde, I said, "Boy, this is one party that is going to be hard to interrupt."

We talked it over and decided that as wonderful as all the teachings were at the convention, we should spend our remaining days in the streets. We would spend our evenings at the worship meetings.

I would return to the Red Light district, but this time in my wedding gown. I would also be armed with my bouquet and invitations in each language as we made our way back to the famous street.

The following day I started my walk alone. This time Heaven opened for me.

Perhaps it was the shock of a woman dressed in a beautiful white flowing gown, so out of place, that interrupted the daily activity. As I stood in front of the women in the windows, each wanted to see me. I was welcomed into each of the window rooms.

In pure delight, I took each girl's hand and said, "I've been sent here by God to tell you that you are not forgotten. He loves you dearly."

As I went from room to room, I got bolder in my witness. I was able to lead the last girl to Christ. As soon as we finished her prayer of acceptance, her pimp grabbed my arm and pulled me outside and down the street away from the dreaded cubicle.

As he pulled me down the street, I yelled out to her, "Don't forget what I said."

"I won't! I won't!" she said.

Someone asked me later what the women looked like.

"They looked like angels."

"Like angels? How could they look like angels?"

I shrugged. "I don't know. I guess I was looking at them through God's eyes."

In the Streets

From then on, we were in the streets every day. It was easy to get flowers; they were on every street corner.

One time, when I was in my gown, we rode a streetcar to town. Everybody on the streetcar broke out in a love song. It was like something out of a movie. For two weeks, I traveled the city in my wedding dress. Locals began to recognize us. People would wave, and some gave me flowers. We had total favor.

One day I ended up in town in my street clothes and needed a place to change, so I went into one of the beautiful empty church cathedrals to put on my gown. When I came out as the Bride of Christ, the local TV news station met me with their cameras rolling.

"What do you have to say to us?" the cameraman said.

I was shocked. Apparently, word had gotten out about what we were doing. But after a moment, I looked right at the camera. "God loves Amsterdam," I said, "and you are all invited to His wedding in Heaven!"

The newspaper also featured us. With hardly any effort on our part, the entire city heard the Good News.

I began to realize just how much God must love the lost of Amsterdam and how, as the Scripture says, He longed to gather his children together as a hen gathers her chicks under her wings (see Matthew 23:37).

12

Spreading the Vision

Holy Ghost Extravaganza!

ONE EVENING WE STAYED LATE witnessing downtown, so instead of going back to the hotel to change clothes, we decided to share our ministry with the evangelists at the convention.

At that point, we had felt so much favor from God that we just couldn't keep it to ourselves any longer. We had to share it with our brothers and sisters.

On this evening, hundreds of African evangelists were walking toward the convention center. It seemed as if at least one-third of the evangelists were from African nations. I don't know where all of them were staying, but they arrived by the busload each night. I stood there facing them in my wedding gown.

At first, people looked at me with a question on their faces. Then Clyde belted out in a loud voice, "The Bride of Christ!"

All of a sudden, everyone stopped in their tracks. Then one man yelled out, "Who told you this?"

Clyde shouted, "The Holy Spirit!"

At that point, all I can remember is everybody went crazy. They were yelling, "Praise God! Hallelujah!"

In seconds the whole parking lot turned into a huge party. It was the Holy Ghost extravaganza! Amidst the praising and jumping up and down, everyone started to dance. Truly the Holy Spirit joined in the party.

Revelation 19:7-8 (NASB) says,

> *Let's rejoice and be glad and give the glory to Him,*
> *because the marriage of the Lamb has come,*
> *and His bride has prepared herself.*
> *It was given to her to clothe herself in fine linen,*
> *bright* and *clean,*
> *for the fine linen is the righteous acts of the saints.*

Sharing the Ministry

In the hope that others would want to share our ministry and take what we had done back to their own countries, I had brought nine wedding gowns to give away. But we were overwhelmed with the response. I didn't know how to choose, but the choice was taken out of my hands. As soon as I opened up my suitcase, we were mobbed.

It was completely crazy! People just started grabbing the dresses and fighting over them. I think I could have brought ten thousand gowns and given each one of them away.

As our time ended at the conference, we still had a few days left, so we decided to go to Paris. After all, we still had our invitations in French. We found a hotel not far from the famous Moulin Rouge.

The next day I was standing under the Eiffel Tower in my wedding gown, inviting people to Heaven with my French invitations. It was truly surreal. If someone had told me six months before that I would be standing under the Eiffel Tower inviting the French to Heaven, I would have said, "You're crazy!"

Little did I realize that was only the beginning of where the Spirit would take His Bride.

I Believe in Them

Never have I felt so close to God as I did spending those two weeks stepping out in faith sharing the gospel. It seemed like He led us every step of the way. It was all orchestrated by Him. Praise God!

I remember one day, as we were sharing our faith in Amsterdam, many of the young people would say they didn't believe in God because of what happened there during World War II. That stumped me.

I asked God, "What do I say to that?"

He said, "You tell them I believe in them!"

And so, I did.

That simple phrase opened up a whole new door of faith. I could see in their eyes that it touched them and perhaps gave them a new way to look at things.

Sweet Reminders

When we returned home to Oregon, we were surprised to find that Billy Graham's *Decision Magazine* did a whole two-page story on us sharing our faith in Amsterdam. It featured a huge picture of Clyde intently sharing his faith with a man in the street who was standing with a bottle of whisky in his hand. The article and picture were a sweet reminder of what it felt like to be used by God to shine His light in the darkness.

> *You are the light of the world.*
> *A city that is set on a hill cannot be hidden.*
> *Nor do they light a lamp and put it under a basket,*
> *but on a lampstand, and it gives light*
> *to all who are in the house.*
> *Let your light so shine before men,*
> *that they may see your good works*
> *and glorify your Father in heaven.*
> —Matthew 5:14-16

Part 4
The Bride's Discovery

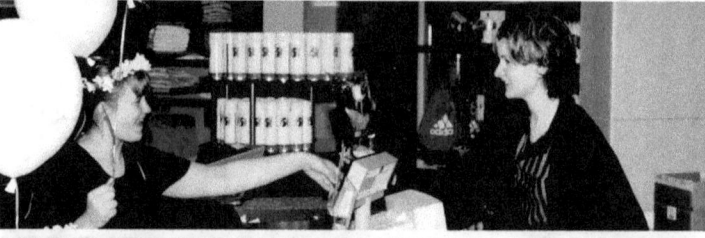

Rogue Valley Mall

January 9, 2003

Dear Debbie:

We are pleased to be the host site for **Rogue Valley Fellowship's Bride Ministries** to be held at the Mall **February 14, 2003**.

Enclosed is a **Promotion Agreement** and **Applicable Operating Rules**.

The **Promotion Agreement and Operating Rules** should be signed and returned to the Mall office prior to the show. Please review the **Applicable Operating Rules** thoroughly. Although you have permission to use the Mall as your event site, it is important that you are aware of and adhere to our criteria for all events.

We also ask that you provide a certificate of insurance with the following listed as additionally insured:

    Rogue Valley Partners, L.P.
    Jones Lang LaSalle Americas, Inc.
    L.P.I. Service Corporation
    GG&A Rogue Valley LLC
    Gregory Greenfield & Associates, Ltd.
    Gregory Greenfield & Associates, Inc.

Please refer to the Promotion Agreement for additional insurance information.

Thanks for your attention to all these details. Please feel free to contact me if you have any further questions or concerns.

Sincerely,

Tesha Lopez
Assistant Marketing Manager

Enclosures

13

Out of the Mouth of Babes

Red Balloons of Jesus' Love

EARLY THE NEXT YEAR, we started thinking about what we wanted to plan next. Valentine's Day was just a few weeks away. Wouldn't it be fun, we thought, to bring Jesus into this special day of honoring love? After all, John 3:16 says,

> For God so loved the world
> that He gave His only begotten Son
> that whosoever should believe in Him
> should not perish but have everlasting life.

But now the question was, "How do we go about such a thing?"

A balloon was the first thing that came to our minds. Not just any balloon, but a special balloon like a mylar balloon in a beautiful red heart shape. And it needed to have a great message with a beautiful font saying something like, "Jesus loves you and wants you in Heaven."

Now you can't just go out and buy balloons like that. They don't exist. So, we had to design them and order them. When we picked out the font in white, it looked so beautiful that we decided to order a thousand.

By this time in our ministry, we had two colossal helium tanks, and after getting them filled and enlisting a handful of volunteers, we headed for Ashland. We blew up our balloons and, two by two, we each took different sections of the town and went into every store, handing every shopkeeper one of our balloons.

We happily told them how God was thinking about them on this special day of love, and most of all, He loves them.

It went so well, and it was so much fun, we decided we would stop in the little towns of Talent and Phoenix on the way back to Medford. We did the same thing in every store in each town and left one of our beautiful balloons at each place, reminding everyone how much they were loved and wanted by God in Heaven.

After three in the afternoon, we decided to meet at our local shopping Mall. We planned to do the same thing in every store. We also planned to give balloons to Valentine's Day shoppers. We had six moms and about ten kids helping us.

Evangel, our local Christian bookstore in the Mall, invited us to use their store as the base to fill our balloons with helium. It was wonderful to see hundreds of balloons being filled up and then watch the excitement of all the kids running in every direction to make sure everyone they saw was carrying a balloon.

The funniest thing happened while we were in the Mall. One of our pastors happened to be shopping for a gift for his wife in the lingerie department of one of the stores. The kids saw him and shouted his name.

He told us later that he went from store to store trying to get away from the kids, but they found him every time. He was in the underwear department when he finally gave up and left the Mall.

Kids and Evangelism

I believe we have too often overlooked the fact that God loves to use kids in evangelism. Their little hearts are so pure, and they haven't yet learned to be stumbled by the fear of man. I can tell you what kid evangelism looks like. With the kid's help, the whole Mall was starting to turn red with our beautiful balloons.

As the kids ran from store to store, one little boy went into Mervyn's and handed a balloon to the cashier.

"Oh, thank you so much," she said.

"You're welcome!" he said with a big smile. Then he said, "Do you know Jesus?"

She said, "No, I don't."

He said, "Would you like to?"

She said, "Yes, I would." And he led her to the Lord right in front of her cash register.

> . . . *Out of the mouths of babes and nursing infants*
> *You have perfected praise* . . .
> —Matthew 21:16

Doing it the Right Way

As I was standing in the middle of the Mall, taking it all in, a man employed by the Mall management marched up to me. He looked furious.

"You and your people have to leave. Right now!"

Oh boy! He was really mad. I felt terrible, because I didn't know what we had done wrong. All I knew was that I was in deep trouble. I gathered all my helpers and left.

The next day, as I was trying to gather my courage to call and apologize, I kept thinking to myself, *how did it go so wrong? It seemed like everyone was so happy!*

It seemed that once again, I had upset the management. Trying to do good seemed to get people mad! This habit was starting to become a common thread in my ministry.

I was afraid to call the Mall to apologize, fearing I would again be yelled at, but I knew I had to. When the Mall manager answered, I said, "I am so sorry. I never meant to do any harm. I thought I was just making people happy."

He told me their side of the story. He explained that because we were handing out balloons in every store and in the common area, our actions became the responsibility of the Mall management.

The manager explained, "What if you had a balloon pop and someone got scared and possibly had a heart attack? We, the Mall management, would have been responsible, and we would have been held accountable."

I said, "Oh, I'm so sorry. I had no idea I was putting you at risk."

I think at that point, I might have even started to cry.

When he realized I was genuinely sorry, he said, "You know, there is a way you could have done it the right way."

"Really? What could that be?"

"You could have a table and the space for what you would like to do and set it up anywhere in the common area as long as you are covered by insurance. Then you are responsible for what you plan to do at your outreach table."

I thanked him, and from then on, with the help of a local church, we were provided with insurance, and we had permission to bring our beautiful Arbor from the float. We set up tables with flowers and candy and anything we wanted to give away with our invitations to Heaven given by the Bride.

Because we had been so well received, we continued to take the Bride Ministry to the Mall on various special occasions such as Mothers Day and Valentine's Day.

Once again, people were intrigued and drawn to see what we offered. We didn't have to go to them; they came to us. It was so beautiful to be able to share the gospel with others. We had total freedom to talk with them, pray with them, encourage them, and show them the love of God through the church.

We took advantage of this new way to reach the lost for Christ. People would often see our Bride standing in the Mall, inviting everyone so that the wedding chamber would be full.

14

She is a Lily

Where's the Wedding?

CHRISTMAS WAS OVER, and of course, I was broke. I don't know what it is, but we moms feel the enormous responsibility to always make every Christmas the best ever. New Year's Eve was now approaching, and Ashland's New Year's celebration was always one colossal party. We knew there would be hundreds of people in the bars and on the streets. Although I was still pretty worn out from Christmas, it wasn't hard to heed the call to the harvest fields on that famous night.

We were pretty much feeling the dead cold of winter, so I wanted to hand out bouquets with our wedding invitations to Heaven. It would be like a breath of warmth and light in a dark season. How that was going to happen didn't seem plausible, especially since we had no money.

With a huge sigh, I decided to do a cold call.

A cold call is where you call someone you don't know and try to convince them to help you in an area that doesn't make sense to the average person. In this case, I would randomly call a florist shop and do my best not to sound like an idiot. I had even heard missionaries say the most challenging part of their ministry was raising support.

So, I took a deep breath and dialed the first number I saw in the phone book.

A lady answered.

As I tried to explain what I was hoping to do, she interrupted me in a manner I thought was kind of harsh.

"Wait a minute," she said. "Are you a Christian?"

"Y-yes," I stammered, hoping we had some common ground but worried we didn't.

"I have a warehouse full of flowers," she said. "And you can have them all!"

At that point, I was picking myself up off the floor. *Did I hear her right?*

She went on to say she owned a famous flower shop in San Francisco, and she had sent her son here to Medford to open up a second store. Unfortunately, her son could not get the business off the ground, so she had him close the business, which left a warehouse full of flowers!

Although I had seen God work many miracles by now, I still found myself in utter awe as I stared at flowers of every season and type that filled her warehouse with unbelievable beauty. It took us two full truckloads to gather them all and bring them home.

Still in shock, as we put the most beautiful bouquets together, I had a hard time believing what God had done before our very eyes. We had close to four hundred bouquets!

The next thing on our agenda was to pick a bridal gown.

Bridal gowns are extremely expensive. Yet, through a series of amazing and miraculous events that only God could have orchestrated, I had acquired, for free, a number of beautiful wedding gowns that I would go on to loan out, for free, to brides who did not have the money to buy their own.

From this cache of wedding gowns, I picked out a beautiful gown to match our beautiful bouquets. Then, around 9:00 p.m. on New Year's Eve, we made our way to Ashland. It was a gloriously cold night. We went from bar to bar, and they were packed with standing room only with a lot of happy people.

At one bar, one woman yelled over all the noise, "Where's the wedding?"

I yelled back, "In Heaven!

And she said, "Oh, my God!"

I said, "Yes! He will be there!"

The whole bar let out a roar of laughter, and everyone seemed delighted to come to the wedding.

God's Lily

At around 2:30 in the morning, we had handed out most of the flowers. When we returned to Medford, we thought we would stop at a few more bars to hand out the rest of the flowers.

We stopped at this little club that was like a dive bar. As I looked around inside, I saw an older woman passed out at a table. She was all alone. My first thought was I didn't want to waste the bouquet on her, because she was passed out.

But, before I could pass her by, I heard the Lord say, "She's a Lily."

I had no idea what that meant, and I was cold and tired by then. *Okay. Whatever.*

I laid the bouquet next to her head. Then I quickly moved on to the other people in the bar until all the bouquets were handed out.

We didn't get home until 4:00 in the morning. As I was taking things from the back of the truck, I saw a tiny bundle of ugly flowers. I just left them there and went into the house.

When I went back out to the truck later that morning, to my surprise, those ugly flowers had opened up during the night. I was shocked to be staring at three lovely lilies.

Suddenly, I remembered the lady who was passed out in the bar. She must have been what God was trying to say. She must have been His lily, and He was looking for her.

Oh, how easy it is to miss the Divine.

But not that night. To me, the three lilies were the Father, the Son and the Holy Ghost. They found her.

> *Like a lily among thorns,*
> *So is my love among the daughters.*
> *—Song of Solomon 2:2*

15

Las Vegas, Dying for Love

Lost Vegas

I HAD NEVER BEEN TO LAS VEGAS, but after being called there, I think the proper title of the town would be more like "Lost Vegas."

Becky, one of the Brides God had called to work with us, was going to Las Vegas because her husband had a business meeting scheduled there. Clyde and I felt God drawing us to meet her there and see what God wanted to do.

I contacted the florist in San Francisco who gave me the warehouse of flowers for New Year's Eve. "You want to pitch in on this adventure?" I asked.

"Oh yes!" she answered. And right away, she flew three hundred long-stemmed roses complete with ferns and Baby's Breath to Vegas for us. I was so excited! I *knew* God had big plans for us.

One of the first things I learned in Las Vegas was never to walk The Strip. It stretches on and on, and there is so much ahead of you to be dazzled by. I could feel the blisters start to form on my feet, and I realized that at some point, we would have to walk back the way we had come.

Only the Beginning

We chose to stay at the Riviera because it was the least expensive hotel and had its own casino below the rooms. Upon receiving the flowers, I asked the maid for extra sheets so I could lay them down on the carpet in our room to make up the bouquets.

As I was in the middle of one of these bouquets, I heard two women arguing outside our room. They were speaking in Spanish, so I had no idea what the problem was.

One of the women was the maid that had given me the sheets. I opened the hotel room door and waved for her to come in, which she did.

I comforted her and then prayed for her. Then I gave her a rose, and I thought, *Boy, this is only the beginning.*

We arranged to meet Becky, our Bride, on the strip the next day. She was beyond stunning in her beautiful wedding gown. She was so breathtaking that people walking by thought she was advertising for some Las Vegas show. They were sure she must be one of the stars.

Gently and powerfully, she shared her faith with everyone who walked by. I was in complete awe as I watched her lead two young girls to the Lord with such beauty and grace right there on the sidewalk. Just like Jesus ministering in the streets.

We spent all day on the streets of Las Vegas, and it was truly a profitable day for the Kingdom of God.

Stopped at the Door

I had also brought a wedding gown, and I thought I should go to the strip clubs located off The Strip. I would go to the dark side of town where tourists were discouraged from visiting. Around 10:00 p.m., while dressed in my gown and armed with roses, I approached the first strip club. As I tried to enter, a huge bouncer stopped me at the door.

"I just want to drop these flowers off for the girls," I said.

He simply looked at me and shook his head. "No," he said. "You are not going in."

"Okay," I said. "Then can I leave these flowers for them?"

Again, he said, "No."

I went to the next club, and the same thing happened. I was confused, because I was so sure God wanted these girls to have our flowers, yet there seemed to be no way to deliver them. It was almost as if the bouncers knew I was coming.

Finally, out of desperation, I asked one of the bouncers, "Can I come in if I pay?"

"No," he said

"Then, can I get in if you pay?" I asked.

He laughed but still said, "No."

It was like they somehow knew ahead of time what I was doing. I couldn't make a surprise attack!

I couldn't understand what was happening. I was so sure this was what God wanted, but I returned to our room without being able to visit a single club. I felt defeated. I didn't realize until later that God was trying to teach me to simply follow him. He had a new plan. I just didn't know what it was yet.

A Change of Plans

I stared at all the roses, feeling depressed, because I couldn't get them out with our beautiful invitations stuffed inside. Then I decided I would go to the casino below our rooms and give a Rose to each of the employees managing the gambling tables. That's when the magic began to happen.

The dealers were like lifeless robots, not like bundles of energy you see in commercials where everybody looks so happy. No one was happy! Instead, everybody looked utterly lifeless and sad. But when I handed each dealer a rose, they came alive! It was amazing.

I went from table to table interrupting the gambling games with a simple gesture of kindness, which somehow acknowledged the dealers as human beings, who, for a moment, were more important than money.

Soon it became apparent that all these employees were desperate to be recognized and seen as people with real feelings.

Soon our roses filled the entire casino.

Earlier I had given roses to all the maids. A maid passed by me with her cart, and there in the top, she proudly displayed the rose.

I was getting pretty excited by now, and I started to hand roses to people playing the slot machines. I gave one woman a rose and, as soon as I did, she hit the jackpot.

She started screaming, "I won! I won! Thanks to you, I won!"

Then another woman discovered the invitation inside her rose, and she started yelling, "Praise the Lord! Praise the Lord! He is here!" She kept saying it over and over, and it rang throughout the entire casino.

We were now drawing a considerable amount of attention. I tried to calm down and be discrete, but by now, I saw it was a little late for that.

Suddenly a man approached me. He was big and burly and looked just like somebody out of a Mafia movie.

"Follow me," he said in a very gruff voice. Then he led me through the casino and into a back room.

I took a deep breath and thought, *Okay. I'm in huge trouble now.*

It was like when I had been kicked out of the Mall back in Oregon. Only this was big time! I stood trembling in the back room, waiting for the reprimand or worse, that I was sure was coming.

Instead, the big man leaned down and looked straight into my eyes. Then with a thick Italian accent, he said, "Thank you for being so kind to my people."

I was speechless.

Then, he went over to a box, grabbed a t-shirt and handed it to me. On the front was a picture of three slot machines with the words beneath, "You're a winner!"

All I could do was smile. I felt as if the favor of God had fallen upon us both. Once again, I was reminded that sin is dying to be interrupted as long as it's done in love.

> ... "Behold! The Lamb of God
> who takes away the sin of the world! ..."
> —John 1:29

16

Out of Africa

A Change of Plans

OUR CHURCH WAS IN THE MIDDLE of planning a missionary trip to Uganda. Of course, upon hearing about it, I felt God was calling me to go. I had already seen God move miraculously in Amsterdam and Paris, and I knew this would be a trip of a lifetime for me. I thought I was more than ready to go.

As the deadline for buying our tickets got closer and closer, I got more and more excited. But so far, our needed support money had not come in. Still, I wasn't really worried, because I often saw God bring in the needed money at the last minute. But this time, the deadline came and went.

I couldn't believe it. How was God allowing me to miss this monumental moment? Wasn't this what He called me to do? I just couldn't let it go. I was convinced God wanted me to go to Uganda as His Bride. But it didn't make any sense. The deadline had already come and gone, and we had no tickets.

Finally, as the departure date was only a few days off, I thought, *Well, at least I have a video of me as the Bride. I can send that to Africa.* I thought that might be the way God wanted me to go—through a video.

But then I was sure I heard God whisper a firm, "No."

I was shocked. Surely, there was a mistake! This was all wrong. But I couldn't deny what I had heard. It was clear God didn't want me to send the video.

A New Bride

The very next day, I met with Joy, my pastor's wife, for lunch at a downtown restaurant. She had her ticket and would be going on the trip to Uganda. I sat across from her.

I'm sorry," I said. "I won't be sending my video with you to take to Africa."

As soon as the words left my mouth, God revealed His will to me.

"It's you!" I said. "God is sending you as His Bride."

This beautiful, reserved, godly woman instantly burst into tears. "Yes," she said quietly. God has been speaking to me about that very thing."

Soon we were both in tears.

I knew this was a massive leap of faith for Joy, and honestly, I was surprised she was willing to take it. She was never one to try to capture the spotlight.

God never took His hands off the wheel; He just had to pry my hands off.

The rest is history. The anointing of the Holy Spirit that fell on Joy turned her into a powerful witness. Everyone could see the glory of God shining through her. She was transformed under the power of the Holy Spirit as she walked through Uganda's streets proclaiming the gospel. She even made the front page of, *The Guardian,* the biggest newspaper in Uganda. It featured a big photo of her in her wedding gown and her arm extended with her finger pointing toward Heaven. The caption below the picture simply said, "Where is the groom?"

In this way, Joy proudly proclaimed Jesus as her Bridegroom.

Out of Africa

I'm happy to say I was out of Africa, but God was in!

I think it's our nature to get ahead of ourselves, especially when we feel we are helping God. My lesson here was to follow the Spirit, letting Him lead at all times. In other words, Father knows best.

How do you know you are following God?

The first clue is never to think you know where He's going. John 12:26 says,

> *If anyone serves Me,*
> *let him follow Me;*
> *and where I am, there My servant will be also.*
> *If anyone serves Me, him My Father will honor.*

Part 5
The Bride's
Joy

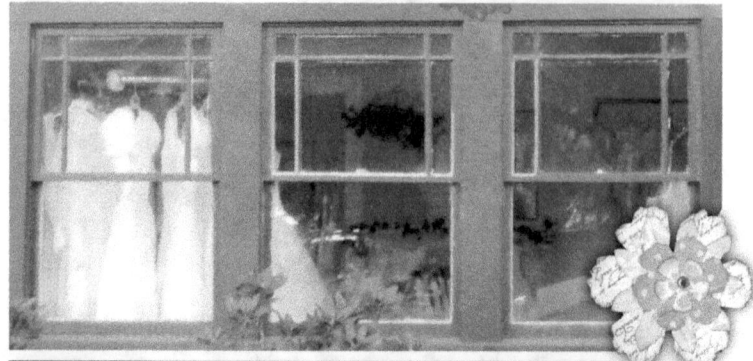

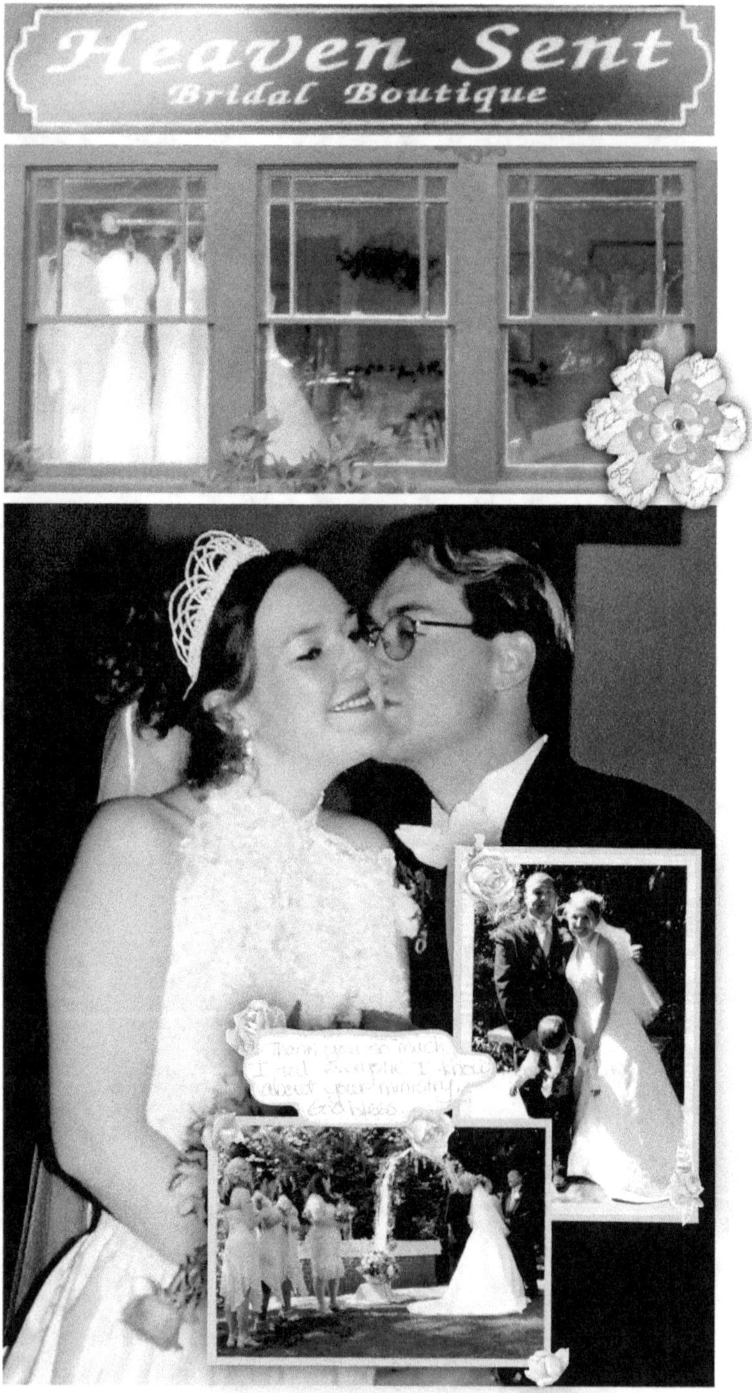
Heaven Sent
Bridal Boutique
Thank you so much
I tell people I know
about your ministry,
God bless.

17

Bridal Boutique

More Than A Dress

IF I HAVE LEARNED ANYTHING from this unique ministry, it is the fact that our God is extravagant, and He is the author of extravagant giving. I believe every woman, if possible, would love to experience a moment in time when their true worth is made manifest. Somehow, the wedding gown plays a huge part in such a discovery.

As I mentioned earlier, through unexpected means, God brought an exceptional number of bridal gowns to me over the years, all for free. It started with a call from a local pastor informing me he was at a yard sale that was selling seven bridal gowns for twenty bucks. Did I want them?

I said yes, not knowing what I would do with them. We had one for our Bride at that time, and it was perfect, so I wasn't looking for more.

Through another ministry we were involved in, we were invited to a Jesus fair where local ministries set up booths sharing what they were doing to serve the Lord. I told the pastor we would be there, and he showed up with the seven gowns. I remember just piling them in a heap in the corner of our booth while thinking I would deal with them later.

A few minutes later, a woman approached our booth and immediately pointed to the gowns. "What are those for?" she asked. She went on to say she was getting married soon and she could not afford a gown.

I told her she was welcome to look at them.

She looked through them and found one she thought was perfect, so she took it into the portable toilets and tried it on. The dress was a perfect fit!

"Take it," I said.

I was instantly overtaken by the overwhelming joy and thankfulness I saw on her face. She was absolutely beaming.

Soon after she walked away, another girl walked up and said almost the same thing as the first girl. I can only assume she saw the other girl walk away with the beautiful gown, because she also said she was getting married and could not afford a dress. She looked through the dresses and found one she loved and that fit.

Once again, I witnessed the sweetness of something I did not expect to be happening. For some reason, it seems like it takes me seeing something twice before I connect the dots.

After two times, I got it. There was a need. A need is what I call the first pull to get you into something deeper. Had I not had those dresses heaped in a pile and witnessed the reaction of those women, this new direction would never have happened. It was the perfect storm that set our feet in a whole new direction.

I immediately wondered how many other women in our area needed a wedding gown but could not afford one.

When I returned home, I had five gowns left and nowhere to display them. With barely any money, we began searching for a shop for a bridal boutique.

The key here is to start the impossible with basically nothing if you want to partner with God. Jesus loves to take a little and turn it into a lot, like the loaves and fishes in Matthew 14:17. Jesus had five loaves to feed 5000 people, and I had five wedding gowns. I was only lacking a couple of fish.

Many people shy away from ministry, because they are unwilling to start unless they have it all, which diminishes the need for God's intervention. I am not saying it's easy to start something with nothing, but it seems to be the way God likes to work. He takes our small desire and gives us twelve baskets left over. I believe He should always play the bigger part in our calling.

Little did I know, back in those early days, that we were going to meet the needs of hundreds of women, not just in a practical way, but in a way that was truly Heaven sent.

Finding a Building

One day, we decided to drive around our town of Jacksonville in search of a building—that we couldn't pay for. We came across a cute little white building right across from the public museum in town. It had once been an ice cream parlor, but it was now closed. The historic building had black-and-white striped awnings over the windows.

I fell in love with it immediately.

When I peeked inside, I saw the beautiful black-and-white tile. The walls were white and extra thick. Apparently, this was where the gold was measured during the gold rush, and the oversized walls were for protection against someone trying to burn the building down. A huge picture window faced the street. It could not have been more perfect.

Now, all we had to do was find the owner.

She was an older woman who owned quite a few buildings in Jacksonville. We explained to her what we hoped to do by the grace of God.

She offered to rent it to us for a very low rate, so we scraped together one month's rent and moved in, trusting God for the rest. This was a leap of faith for us. This was way before anyone ever thought of GoFundMe.

Clyde was a great carpenter, and he built a beautiful counter and countertop. Soon the little ice cream parlor was transformed into an upscale bridal shop where we loaned everything for free.

I'm happy to say that just as fast as bad news gets around, so does good news. Our first bride came to us from a local ministry called Living Alternatives that encouraged pregnant women who were considering getting an abortion to keep their babies. A young woman came to them in tears, saying if her pregnancy test were positive, she would not keep the baby.

The young woman was lost and confused. Her boyfriend had left her, and she was pretty much on her own.

Through the love and support of Living Alternatives, she decided to keep her baby. In time, the volunteers led her to the Lord. Soon after that, she and her boyfriend reconciled, and he also accepted the Lord. They decided to get married.

This young woman came to me hoping that I would have a beautiful gown for her. Unfortunately, the five I had did not fit her.

I was beside myself with anxiety and so sad that I had my first bride but no dress to fit her.

That night, while shopping in one of our local grocery stores, I ran into a friend. I told her about my dilemma. To my surprise, she had a dress she had picked up at Goodwill for one of her relatives who recently got married. She promised to bring it to me the next day.

I got hold of the soon-to-be bride, and she returned to our shop. To our amazement, it was a perfect fit! She looked absolutely beautiful.

God reaffirmed to me that He was truly with us. The perfect dress was just one of many more miracles to come. Over time, more and more women donated their wedding dresses and other items to us until, at one point, I had over 100 gowns, along with shoes, veils, flower girl dresses, jewelry and more. It was so magical! Countless women were blessed to find a beautiful dress for their wedding and at no cost to them.

It's sad, but I have often seen women struggling with their self-worth, which creates a low standard of how they should be treated due to the lack of respect for themselves. I'm not saying a wedding dress is a cure-all, but it's a privilege many women have been denied. Many have never been able to go into a beautiful bridal boutique and pick out the perfect dress of their dreams. And what a joy to top it off with the perfect shoes and veil to complete the picture of her true value and worth.

I remember saying so many times, "You are a princess. Look at you! Just look at you!"

Each time, I hoped the bride-to-be would remember this moment and set high standards of how they will be treated in the future.

The old saying, "Moms are the last ones to get a new pair of shoes," is true. Once you have your children, your life is threaded in sacrifice. Because of this, I believe a woman's special moment at her bridal shop is a rite of passage that should be available to all women, simply for the glory of God.

That's why I opened a bridal boutique that offered everything for free!

A Big Mistake

I'm willing to admit I was so moved time and time again serving these incredible women that I missed what I believe God was trying to tell me. Our little shop got a lot of attention. It soon felt as if we were becoming one of the main attractions when people visited Jacksonville. Everybody, it seemed, wanted to see the free bridal shop.

One day, two beautiful women of God came in to visit, and they were so moved they asked if they could be a part of this outreach.

I'm ashamed to admit I was having so much fun I didn't want to share it. I said, "Thank you so much, but I don't need any help at this time."

Now I've come to believe that was a big mistake.

In any move of God, we must be openhanded with His vision. His purposes are meant to be shared to further the building of His Kingdom. He longs to bring people into His work.

*Then He said to His disciples,
"The harvest truly is plentiful,
but the laborers are few.
Therefore pray the Lord of the harvest
to send out laborers into His harvest."*
—Matthew 9:37-38

Looking for Revival

Many women who came in looking for a wedding gown were not affiliated with a church, and quite a few of them ended up in backyard weddings, repeating their vows from someone who spent a dollar to join the Universal Church of God via the Internet.

I would love to invite local churches to be a part of this ministry. How wonderful if churches would give up space for a beautiful bridal shop in one of their buildings.

It was interesting when the bride-to-be would come into my shop. She would usually bring all her family members to share in her special moment. When I met the new bride, I was often introduced to her entire family.

I understand that many churches will only marry church members, but that leaves out half the town. How wonderful would it be to offer free counseling and open our doors to marry these couples who have no church.

I often hear believers praying for revival, but I think revival is a gift to the unsaved. Ezra 9:8 (NIV) says,

> *But now, for a brief moment,*
> *the LORD our God has been gracious*
> *in leaving us a remnant*
> *and giving us a firm place in his sanctuary,*
> *and so our God gives light to our eyes*
> *and a little relief in our bondage.*

I hope Heaven Sent Bridal Boutiques will pop up all across the country, led by God-fearing women. Truly, if you build it, they will come.

An Abundance

I had been given such an abundance of wedding gowns that I was able to send them out as gifts to missionaries across the world. I even had the privilege of sending a beautiful gown to Iraq in the green zone, the most common name for the International Zone of Baghdad. Here is the letter I received from the head chaplain:

Dear Debbie,

I wanted to write to thank you for the wedding gown that arrived here at the Coalition Provisional Authority, Baghdad, Iraq. It was very kind and thoughtful of you to send it to us for the use in the weddings we perform here in the chapel.

I believe that I mentioned to you that we had a wedding here on December 3, 2003. It was a wonderful event and would have been even lovelier if the bride had been able to dress in a beautiful gown.

We had a second wedding here a week ago between an American civilian contractor and an Iraqi woman. Since she is from Baghdad, she was able to get a wedding gown in the city. However, I have been approached by other American couples who wish to get married and are not able to travel into the city for security reasons. The dress will be perfect for these brides.

Again, I thank you for your kindness, thoughtfulness and generosity for providing our Religious Support Office with the lovely dress. Please know that you will be in our thoughts and prayers.

> *Frank E Wisner, Coalition Provisional Authority Chaplain Baghdad, Iraq.*

18

Jerusalem

The Feast of Tabernacles

EACH ONE OF US HAS EXPERIENCED phenomenal moments in our lives that we wouldn't mind living over and over again.

It was late August. We were slowly saying goodbye to the hot days of summer. We had received an invitation from a private party to travel to Jerusalem to participate in the Feast of Tabernacles. Christians come from around the world to celebrate Jesus during the eight days of The Feast. There was also a special parade in which I would march and represent the Bride of Christ.

The Feast of Tabernacles, also known as the Feast of Booths or Sukkot, is the seventh and last Feast the Lord commanded Israel to observe. It is also one of the three Feasts that Jews were to observe each year.

> *. . . appear before the LORD your God*
> *in the place which He chooses . . .*
> —Deuteronomy 16:16

The importance of the Feast of Tabernacles can be seen in the number of places it is mentioned in Scripture. For one thing, it was at this time that Solomon's Temple was dedicated to the Lord. (See 1 Kings 8.)

It was also at the Feast of Tabernacles that the Israelites, who had returned to rebuild the temple, gathered together to hear Ezra proclaim the word of God to them (Nehemiah 8). Ezra's preaching resulted in a great revival as the Israelites confessed their sin and repented. It was also during this Feast that Jesus said,

> *. . . If anyone thirsts, let him come to Me and drink.*
> *He who believes in Me, as the Scripture has said,*
> *out of his heart will flow rivers of living water.*
> —John 7:37-38

The Feast of Tabernacles, like all the Feasts, was instituted by God to remind every generation of Israelites of their deliverance by God from Egypt. But for us believers, the Feasts foreshadow the work and actions of our coming Messiah. Much of Jesus' public ministry took place in conjunction with the holy Feasts set forth by God.

Most Christian scholars agree that the Feast of Tabernacles is symbolic of Christ's second coming when He will establish His earthly kingdom. Some also believe it is likely that Jesus was born during the Feast of Tabernacles. The Feast of Tabernacles begins and ends with a special day of rest.

During the days of the Feast, all native Israelites are to dwell in booths or huts known in Hebrew as Sukkot. Doing so reminds them that God delivered them out of the land of Egypt and took them forward to the coming Messiah who would deliver His people from the bondage of sin.

Like all the Feasts of Israel, The Feast of Tabernacles consistently reminded the Jews (and also Christians) that God has promised to deliver His people from bondage and sin and that He will deliver them from all their enemies. Part of God's deliverance for the Israelites was His protection of them for the forty years they wandered in the wilderness, cut off from the promised land.

The same holds true for us Christians today. God protects us and provides for us as we go through life in the wilderness of this world. While our hearts long for the promised land and to be in the presence of God, He preserves His own in this world as we await the world-to-come and the redemption that will come when Jesus Christ returns to tabernacle, or as the Scripture says, "to dwell," among us in bodily form.

The New Testament describes Jesus as attending the temple service Sukkot. Zechariah foretold the time when all nations would ascend to Jerusalem each year.

> *All who survive of all those nations*
> *that came up against* Yerushalayim
> *shall make a pilgrimage year by year*
> *to bow low to the King, the Lord of Hosts,*
> *and to observe the Festival of* Sukkot.
> —Zechariah 14:16 *(The Israel Bible)*

It was a great privilege for me to be asked to take part in this pilgrimage while in Jerusalem. On the third day of the Feast, Christians, who had gathered from all nations to celebrate Jesus, would be given an opportunity to march through the streets of Jerusalem in their native dress.

The parade would be a dazzling display of flags from around the world, giving believers from over a hundred countries a chance to march in declaration of our love for Jerusalem. I would march to declare my love for my Bridegroom as the Bride of Christ.

Touching Holy Ground

Sometimes I wonder if we really know what is in our hearts of our love for God. I know we are to live by faith, but in being able to travel to Israel, in my heart of hearts, I wondered if I would be able to feel His presence in a new way. So many times, I remember seeing many of my friends coming home from their visits to Israel with a holy glow about them. How I longed to experience that personally.

I was about to find out.

I certainly had plenty of time to question and think this thought through on the long plane ride. I have a really short attention span, and I began to have doubts. What if I didn't feel anything different? What would that mean?

But as soon as my feet hit the ground in Israel, I knew something was different.

So, this is why they call it the Holy Land.

Have you ever known somebody for a long time, yet they never invited you over to their house? You know them, but there is an intimacy that is missing. A part of their life has been kept from you, even if it is simply daily living. Knowledge of where someone lives, how they live, and where they spend most of their life is meaningful.

I felt that way the minute I touched ground in Israel. It was as if Jesus took my hand and said, "Now I want you to see where I lived."

I woke the first morning to the sound of two birds singing outside my bedroom window. It was like Jesus was saying, "Here are My birds. Don't they sing beautifully?"

I was now listening to what He had heard, and *everything* became my personal pilgrimage. I walked where He walked. I was in His city, and His presence was everywhere.

My prayers ceased to be a one-way conversation. Instead, they became intimate talks. The first night, I put my hand on the holy wall (Western Wall). As my vocabulary became too limited for my spirit, I began to converse in tongues and sing in my Heavenly language.

An Israeli woman was standing next to me at the wall, and she happened to be on her cell phone. When she heard me singing, she told her friend, "I have to go. I must hear what this lady is saying."

My heart was simply overjoyed, and my cup was spilling over. I think I might have splashed on a few people here and there.

Walking in the Footsteps of Jesus

By now, I had walked in the streets of many places and countries, declaring my love for my Bridegroom. But now I was about to walk where His feet once walked. As the day approached, English had now become my second language. My Heavenly language had become number one.

The Feast of Tabernacles is a time of declaring and speaking great truths. I was so excited as I was putting on my wedding gown, knowing I was about to declare my love for Jesus and His Bride to the whole city of Jerusalem. My wedding invitations were written in Hebrew, and I had one gripped in my hand as I lined up with all the Christians preparing to march in the parade.

Jerusalem

Two women approached me and anointed my head with oil as they began to pray over me. At this point, a Heavenly Presence had fallen over me, and it was all I could do to stay on my feet.

How could this be that me, of all people, could have the privilege of standing before God proclaiming His Scripture?

> *Let us be glad and rejoice, and give honour to him:*
> *for the marriage of the Lamb is come,*
> *and his wife hath made herself ready.*
> *And to her was granted*
> *that she should be arrayed in fine linen,*
> *clean and white:*
> *for the fine linen is the righteousness of saints.*
> *And he saith unto me,*
> *Write, Blessed are they which are called*
> *unto the marriage supper of the Lamb.*
> *And he saith unto me,*
> *These are the true sayings of God.*
> *—Revelation 19:7-9 (KJV)*

As we began to march through the streets of Jerusalem, my right hand was raised straight to Heaven with my invitation.

> *And the Spirit and the bride say, Come.*
> *And let him that heareth say, Come.*
> *And let him that is athirst come.*
> *And whosoever will,*
> *let him take the water of life freely.*
> *—Revelation 22:17 (KJV)*

While we marched around the Tower of David, I could almost hear Jesus proclaiming,

> *... If anyone thirsts, let him come to Me and drink.*
> *He who believes in Me, as the Scripture has said,*
> *out of his heart will flow rivers of living water.*
> —John 7:37-38

Rivers of life flowed through me on that day, and the Spirit and the Bride spoke the same language.

As the parade was coming to a close, an Israeli woman ran to me with her daughter, asking me to pray for her. I put my hands on her head and asked God to help her and pour His love upon her. I felt His joy flowing through my fingers.

God was once again touching His people on His streets.

Glory to God!

The Spirit and the Bride say come.
Revelation 22:17

How beautiful are the feet of those who bring good news
Romans 10:15

19

The Bridegroom

Joy Made Full

> *He who has the bride is the groom;*
> *but the friend of the groom,*
> *who stands and listens to him,*
> *rejoices greatly because of the groom's voice.*
> *So, this joy of mine has been made full.*
> —John 3:29 (NASB)

IN THE ABOVE PASSAGE, John the Baptist is lovingly referring to Jesus as the Bridegroom. He states in the very beginning that the fervent love Christ has for His church can only be compared to the love between a bride and her groom.

After the engagement has been accepted, which I believe happens when we ask Christ into our hearts, our true love story begins.

> *. . . if you confess with your mouth the Lord Jesus*
> *and believe in your heart*
> *that God has raised Him from the dead,*
> *you will be saved.*
> —Romans 10:9

When we give our hearts to Christ, the true preparations for the wedding begin. Once the Bride has given her heart, she is engaged.

Have you ever spent time with one of your friends who has just gotten engaged? I'm sure you will agree that her mind is on one thing and one thing only—getting ready for the day of her wedding. Not even an upcoming tidal wave could detour her thoughts.

Fasting

Now, I don't want to get too spiritual here. I just want to have some fun with these comparisons. Have you ever noticed how future brides instinctively put a lot of effort into themselves as they prepare to look their very best? This thrust of improvement is often materialized in diet and fasting to ensure there's no problem fitting into that perfect size wedding gown.

It's interesting in Mark 2:19-20 Jesus says,

> *Can the friends of the bridegroom fast*
> *while the bridegroom is with them?*

As long as they have the bridegroom with them
they cannot fast.
But the days will come
when the bridegroom will be taken away from them,
and then they will fast in those days.

In preparing for our wedding, it is acceptable to deny ourselves by not just working on our outer beauty but also on our inner beauty, allowing ourselves to be adorned in good works. We, as the church, are waiting to see the Bridegroom, and as we wait, we too will fast as the Bride sacrifices to look her best on that special day.

Delivering Invitations

Another important duty of the Bride is to send out invitations to all her family and friends. Once she has made a list of everybody she wants to attend, she turns to her groom and says, "Who is on your list to come to our wedding? Who would you like me to invite on your behalf?"

Jesus answers with three words, "*The whole world.*"

John 3:16 says,

For God so loved the world
that He gave His only begotten Son,
that whoever believes in Him
should not perish but have everlasting life.

This will be a pretty big undertaking, but the honor to invite the whole world on His behalf is set before her. Revelation 22:17 so beautifully gives us (the Bride) the honor of giving out the invitation.

> *And the Spirit and the bride say, "Come!"'*
> *And let him who hears say, "Come."*
> *And let him who thirsts come.*
> *Whosoever desires,*
> *let him take the water of life freely.*

What a beautiful picture of the Bride holding the invitation with her outstretched arm, beckoning all to come.

Preparing a Place

If you are wondering what the Bridegroom has been doing all this time, he has been preparing a special surprise for His Bride. He is going to take her someplace so wonderful that,

> *. . . as it is written, "Eye has not seen, nor ear heard,*
> *Nor have entered into the heart of man*
> *The things which God has prepared*
> *for those who love Him."*
> —1 Corinthians 2:9

That certainly sounds like some honeymoon! It cannot even be expressed in words.

The Bridegroom

Not only is our bridegroom preparing for our honeymoon, but He is also busy preparing a place for his Bride to live permanently. Jesus says,

> *In My Father's house are many mansions;*
> *if it were not so, I would have told you.*
> *I go to prepare a place for you*
> *...I will come again and receive you to Myself;*
> *that where I am, there you may be also.*
> *—John 14:2-3*

Is the Bridegroom calling you right now?

Why not make absolutely certain of Heaven by opening your heart to Christ the Savior and Lord? Right now, invite Him to enter, to cleanse your heart from sin, and make it His permanent dwelling place.

He gives us this assurance,

> *... If anyone hears My voice and opens the door,*
> *I will come in to him and dine with him,*
> *and he with Me.*
> *—Revelation 3:20*

> *... Holy, holy, holy*
> *Lord God Almighty,*
> *Who was and is and is to come!*
> *—Revelation 4:8*

20

Going Forward

Not the End of the Story

THERE ARE MANY WAYS to share the Gospel. I hope to encourage and broaden your imagination. By being faithful with little, God will truly trust us with much!

My Heaven Sent Bridal Shop is just a small glimpse into the many ministries I have started or been involved in. Ashland Community Radio (KSKQ) contacted me and asked me to come and speak about The Bride Outreach.

After the show, the man interviewing me asked if I would like to host a show on their station.

The station hosts shows of all different genres. My show was called "For the Joy." David, a friend of mine and fellow Christian, was my engineer. I interviewed almost every nonprofit in the valley. We played Christian music and shared our faith, which was a first for that station.

On one show, I interviewed the man in charge of Medford Gospel Mission, a place that helps the homeless and other down-and-out people. Their mission statement is "Relief, Restoration, Transformation."

When I heard about this wonderful idea of reaching the lost with love and kindness, I felt led to join the Mission in this service. I have served there ever since and am going on my ninth year of volunteering with them.

In the past three years, I have led a popsicle ministry every summer. I give out free popsicles to all the kids on my street and beyond, along with a pop-up Bible promise card designed by pastor and author P.K. Hallinan. Sometimes I have had as many as ten kids at a time at my door!

It is so sweet to watch the kids as they close their eyes and pick a promise out of the basket and then read it aloud. Those are truly heartfelt moments.

Halloween night, 2019, I once again put on a wedding gown and visited the town of Ashland, inviting all who were out that night to my wedding in Heaven.

> *Therefore go into the highways,*
> *and as many as you find, invite to the wedding.*
> *So those servants went out into the highways*
> *and gathered together all whom they found,*
> *both bad and good.*
> *And the wedding hall was filled with guests.*
> —Matthew 22:9-10

God will use each and every one of us who ask Him to do so, not just when we are young but even into and through old age.

I am not a hard act to follow. I am as simple as they come. I have never written a book before. I have no college degrees to brag about. I am just a believer who became a seeker. By the grace of God, I found a purpose for my life as God led me step-by-step to follow in His footsteps. He led me to his Fountain of Joy, where His living water flows.

And He can do the same for you.

I would have never dreamed, when I started out those many years ago, that God would use me in so many diverse ways and that He would inspire and use me in so many types of ministries. But, my friends, this is not the end of the story . . . that's for another book . . . should the Lord tarry.

Debbie Hicks

spiritandthebride@hotmail.com

The Spirit and the Bride say Come!"

Let us be glad and rejoice, and give honour to him:
For the marriage of the Lamb is come,
and his wife hath made herself ready.

And to her was granted that she should be arrayed in fine linen,
clean and white: for the fine linen is the righteousness of saints.

And he saith unto me, Write, Blessed are they which are called
unto the marriage supper of the Lamb.
And he saith unto me, these are the true sayings of God.
—Revelation 19:7-9 (KJV)

And the Spirit and the bride say, Come! And let him that heareth
say, Come. And let him that is athirst come. And whosoever will,
let him take the water of life freely.
—Revelation 22:17 (KJV)

Why not make absolutely certain of Heaven
by opening your heart to Christ, the Savior and Lord?
Right now, invite Him to enter, to cleanse it from sin,
and to make it His personal dwelling place.
He gives us this assurance:

If anyone hears My voice and opens the door,
I will come in to him and dine with him, and he with Me.
—Revelation 3:20

Who was - - - and is - - - and is to come!
—Revelation 4:8

ACKNOWLEDGMENTS

Clyde, you know if it hadn't been for you, we would have never left the park. Our beautiful float turned into a glimpse of Heaven. So many doors were opened, and so many hearts were touched because of your passion and your love of God for the lost. You worked tirelessly on everything. Thank you for making this dream a reality. You are a true visionary, and God trusted you to carry the Bride across the globe! Thank you for your great leadership. Glory to God!

Jan, I can't thank you enough for the countless hours you spent on my behalf. Your encouragement was so very helpful, not to mention all the typing. This book was certainly an adventure and a learning experience that you turned into a labor of love. I so appreciate you believing that these stories need to be told. So many times, your faith and belief in these stories kept me going. You are so dear to me. Thank you so much!

Over the years, God raised up His army of faithful women and children and brothers who were not afraid but full of joy to be His witnesses! I'm so blessed and overwhelmed seeing all of you coming alongside the beautiful float as we went from city to city, sharing the Good News of Jesus coming for His Bride.

We so happily became His servants as we invited the bad and the good (Matthew 22:10), so His wedding would be full. It was an honor and a privilege for me to walk side by side with all of you. I thank you all from my heart.

We participated in forty-one parades from one end of the state to the other, inviting every town to Heaven!

Many of you will recognize these stories, because you took part in them. I fear that if I start naming names, I will leave one of you out. So, I would like to thank all of you for your kindness, faith and love. Your reward is in Heaven. And please know that this book could not have been written without you. My stories are your stories.

God Bless You All,

Debbie

ABOUT THE AUTHOR

Debbie has a gift for hearing God as He leads her in discovering many ways to beautifully serve Him through serving others. She is passionate about sharing her discoveries with others of like heart. It's not unusual to hear her say something like, "If God can use me, He can use anybody."

She currently resides in Southern Oregon, where she has lived for more than thirty years. Two grown children and one adorable grandchild fill Debbie's world with delight. She shares her home with a few cats, and she shares her backyard with five ducks, two chickens, and several friendly goats.

Debbie loves making everything in her world beautiful and uses her amazing green thumb to nurture an incredible array of thriving plants and trees.

The Spirit and the Bride say Come! is Debbie's first book.

Contact

Debbie Hicks
spiritandthebride@hotmail.com

www.needlerockpress.com
for future books!

Reviews are like gold to authors.
If you have enjoyed this book,
please consider leaving a review
on Amazon or Goodreads
or
share on your
favorite social media.
Thanks so much!

www.ingramcontent.com/pod-product-compliance
Lightning Source LLC
Chambersburg PA
CBHW072017110526
44592CB00012B/1348